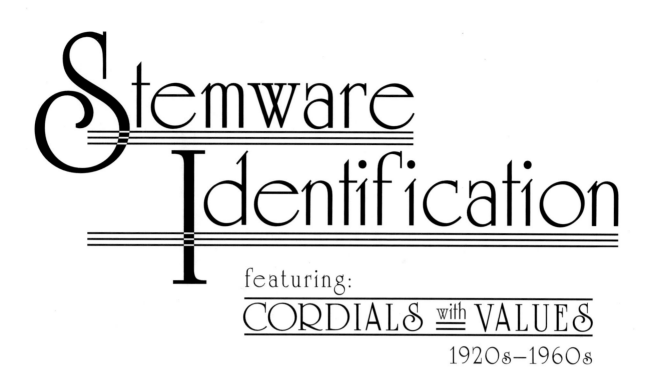

Stemware Identification

featuring:
CORDIALS with VALUES

1920s–1960s

Gene Florence

COLLECTOR BOOKS
A Division of Schroeder Publishing Co., Inc.

The current values in this book should be used only as a guide. They are not intended to set prices, which vary from one section of the country to another. Auction prices as well as dealer prices vary greatly and are affected by condition as well as demand. Neither the Author nor the Publisher assumes responsibility for any losses that might be incurred as a result of consulting this guide.

Searching For A Publisher?

We are always looking for knowledgeable people considered to be experts within their fields. If you feel that there is a real need for a book on your collectible subject and have a large comprehensive collection, contact Collector Books.

Cover Design: Beth Summers
Book Design: Benjamin R. Faust

Printed in the U.S.A. by Image Graphics, Paducah, KY

Acknowledgments

I have been fortunate to have many people help me put my books together. Cathy, my wife has always been involved in sorting, packing, and unpacking the glass, both at home and at the photography sessions, plus editing each of my sixty books; and although she no longer types them, she makes sure that they are easily understood by anyone whether they have knowledge about the glass or not. However, this book may not have begun had it not been for her persistence in wanting me to pursue it.

She spent days helping me search for the mystery stems that were eluding identification. Each stem was photographed individually, and we had to search through over 800 transparencies in order to place them in the proper spot in the book. Cathy rigged a light box so we could view fifty to ninety transparencies at once, using a book case, Plexiglas, a shower curtain, and florescent lights. It saved $1,000 over ordering one, worked well, and is portable! It camped in the middle of the floor for a month while we were using it daily! No words can thank her enough for the work she does in the background!

All the individual transparencies were taken by Charley Lynch who is the official photographer for Collector Books. He normally likes to take individual pictures, but he gasped and moaned once he saw I had forty-eight feet of table space covered in cordials to be recorded. In all, it took a couple of months (with several being reshot) to perfect patterns; but he did it. Thanks, Charley!

Many dealers have aided the cordial cause over the years. I would particularly like to thank Dick and Pat Spencer, Dan Tucker and Lorrie Kitchen, Lynn Welker, Kevin Kiley, Swede and Kay Larsson, and John and Evelyn Knowles for thinking of me when they found interesting cordials. Dan has also hauled back many pieces of glass for me when I flew to shows.

The following have assisted me by lending or identifying stems and submitting prices for the cordials in this book: Lynn Welker, Dick and Pat Spencer, Leroy and Susan Allen, Bob Page, Dale Frederiksen, Roy and Doris Isaacs, Kelly O'Kane, Matt Ellenberg, Joe and Florence Solito, Cliff and Lydia O'Neil, Glen Everett, and Ken Butler. Special thanks go to Bob Page and Dale Frederiksen of Replacements, Inc. for allowing me to spend a day there using their catalogs of information. Both of them took time from their busy schedules to personally help me identify some unknown stems. They are particularly knowledgeable about companies on which they have published books. Their books are listed in the bibliography on page 157. If you are ever in the Greensboro, NC, area, Replacements is worth a visit!

The staff at Collector Books has worked tirelessly on this book. Della Maze and Charley Lynch helped set up data base entry files so we could have a way to enumerate and communicate each of the 648 cordials pictured in this book to the staff as well as you. The editing staff are non-collectors; most of these stems look the same to them. When I needed a particular stem placed in one of nine spots on a page, it was critical for people in Paducah to know which stem I referred to while I wrote in Florida. Also thanks to Benjamin Faust on the Collector Books staff for the layout of this book.

Both Billy Schroeder and Lisa Stroup of Collector Books saw more cordials and transparencies of cordials than they probably wish to ever see again. Billy worked on arranging all the pictures in numerical order only to find at finish that not all were correct! Bummer! We discovered some cordials were pictured twice with different numbers. At first, there were 876 photos to coordinate!

After photography, Lisa had to pack each cordial and make sure it was numbered on the outside, too, so we could find it again if any problems arose. They did; and she had to find several to reshoot! In general, you needed to be there to comprehend the years that went into this book! I've tried to give you an idea of our tasks these last eight months that have often been a detriment to sanity; but other than that...!

Preface

This book had its beginnings in the middle of the 1970s when a fellow dealer/collector, Walt Brown, died leaving his cordial collection to his wife, Sarah. She contacted me (because I had recently started buying cordials) and wanted to know if I would be interested in acquiring Walt's collection of 300+ cordials for possible use in a book. She wanted the years of Walt's work not to have been in vain... to ensure his interest a certain longevity. She sent me a list and a price was set to both our satisfactions. That is how I seriously got hooked on buying these little liqueur glasses. As a non-drinker, I had to look up what a cordial was when I first heard the term! Actually, the best explanation I ever heard was that a cordial was a stemmed shot glass that gave high society an excuse to have a shot away from the lowly neighborhood bar.

Space to display glass was at a premium in our small house and I mistakenly thought cordials would only take up "a little area." I never realized how many I would eventually acquire over the years nor how many varieties there are floating about in our society! In actuality, they were never all unpacked or displayed at one time until last year when they were carted to Paducah to photograph.

Word had leaked out over the years that I was going to do a cordial book because I bought them. That was only a distant consideration. Cordials seemed like too limited an area to do a book even though there were hundreds of collectors beginning to accumulate these little stems. As time went by, I realized that water goblets would have been more suited for use in a stemware book; but they took up more display room.

I ultimately had to set limits for my purchases. I determined to buy only cordials made by major glass companies; but I kept finding some neat looking stems that seemed to beckon me. Many of those "neat" cordials have plagued me over the last eight months as I have tried in vain to find out who made them! Anyone who has ever searched to identify one unknown stem can multiply that futility many times over as Cathy and I have turned thousands of pages trying to find out the manufacturer of just one more stem pictured in this book.

I received encouragement from several friends in the glass business to follow through on this book as a stemware guide. Some said something to the effect of a sarcastic "Good luck!" Most of the time those statements were followed by eyes rolled back in the head. As I sit here at my computer in early June, I have missed the opening of both the Morgantown and Fostoria conventions, an annual pilgrimage; and I have to leave for the Heisey convention in two days! I'm running out of hours to finish this book (before it finishes me)!

I had set a tentative deadline of early May, so I could do some shellcracker fishing before I returned to Kentucky. I'm now working in Kentucky and all the fish are still safe in Florida! I knew this would not be easy; but I misjudged how much time would go into this book. In the past, I had considered selling the collection; now, as this task winds down, I'm of two minds about that! Mostly I'm glad that I still had them, have a few more to find, and am sharing them with you!

Pricing

ALL PRICES IN THIS BOOK ARE FOR MINT CONDITION CORDIALS ONLY. This book is to be used for identification of your stems. Please realize that cordials are usually the most expensive stem in any stemware line. I wish I could give you a general guide for pricing other stems in the lines shown in this book. I know that some other books do that; but pricing does not work that way.

You cannot say that a wine is always 50% of the cordial price when it can be 75% in one line and 110% in another! I wish pricing were so simple, but it is not! I defy anyone to tell you that it is! The few I've run across espousing that theory do not price their own merchandise that way when they go to sell it!

Measurements

All measurements in this book are to the nearest $\frac{1}{16}$". No catalog listings or sales listings of glassware have been used. Each stem has been carefully measured and dutifully recorded. Errors may have occurred some place in the process, but attempts have been made to assure this book is as accurate as humanly possible. Height measurements will vary as much as $\frac{1}{4}$" due to mold changes or quality of craftmanship over the years.

Contents

Glass Companies Represented

Anchor-Hocking/Hocking Glass Company, Lancaster, OH
Astral, New York, NY
Bryce Brothers Company, Mt. Pleasant, PA
Cambridge Glass Company, Cambridge, OH
Canton Glass Company, Marion, IN
Central Glass Works, Wheeling, WV
Dorflinger Glass Company, White Mills, PA
Duncan & Miller Glass Company, Washington, PA
Economy Glass Company, Morgantown, WV
Fostoria Glass Company, Moundsville, WV
H. C. Fry Company, Rochester, PA
Glastonbury Glass Company, Chicago, IL
T. G. Hawkes Glass Company, Corning, NY
Heisey Glass Company, Newark, OH
Huntington Tumbler Company, Huntington, WV

Imperial Glass Company, Bellaire, OH
Lancaster Glass Company, Lancaster, OH
Libbey Glass Manufacturing Company, Toledo, OH
Glastonbury/Lotus Glass Company, Barnesville, OH
McKee Glass Company, Jeannette, PA
Morgantown Glass Works, Morgantown, WV
New Martinsville Glass Company, New Martinsville, WV
Paden City Glass Manufacturing Company, Paden City, WV
Seneca Glass Company, Morgantown, WV
Steuben Glass Works, Corning, NY
Tiffin Glass Company, Tiffin, OH
Utility Glass Works, Lonaconing, MD
Westmoreland Glass Company, Grapeville, PA
West Virginia Specialty Company, Star City, WV

How to Use This Book

I've mulled over the layout of a book like this for several years. My goal was to try to save the time of going through book after book trying to identify a stem. This book will not try to distinguish every known stem, but it will help you to identify many of those you find in the marketplace. This book used my cordials as a starting point. After twenty years of gathering them, I finally have an opportunity of using them for a greater advantage than just occupying less space than a goblet collection! I hope to expand this book every two or three years as the need arises. You will be able to tell what I need to add by what is not shown! If you have an identified stem not shown, let me know. By the same token, if you know what any of the unidentified stems are in this book, please drop me a line.

I considered arranging the stems by company for a while, but if you know the company, you probably do not need this book! The logical way seemed to be by color, since most people can distinguish colors.

Any stem with amber should be looked for in the Amber section whether it is all amber, amber foot, or amber bowl. However, if it is amber and some other color such as amber and green, look in the Bi-Color section. If not in those sections, you then have to search through the other sections to see if it might be there — but in crystal or another color.

In discussing the stems on a page they are arranged thusly:

All shades of blue will be in the Blue section whether light blue or dark blue; so start your search there. Each colored section is arranged by company alphabetically and line numbers are arranged numerically within a company's listing. Unidentified stems (those which I was unable to document) are under U in the company list of each color. A few of those were authenticated after the book's pages of nine cordials were laid (in stone) for printer color separations. These will be listed in the Unidentified section of each color (even though some are identified now). Sorry! Believe me, the hundreds of hours spent on this book will never be totally appreciated!

Look at the Contents for the section listings. If a stem is iridized, there is a section for that and if it has a metallic stem, there is one for that.

The Crystal section is broken into several categories to (hopefully) simplify searching. If a stem is crystal only, look in the Crystal section. If it has a cut pattern, then look under Crystal Cut for it. If it has an etching, then look under Crystal Etch. Crystal sections also include Crystal Frosted, and Crystal with Platinum, Silver, or Gold. Seek your crystal category first. The big question for most collectors is how to distinguish cut from etch. There is not a simple explanation and many long-time collectors and dealers have a problem with this; so here goes my brief explanation.

An etch is done with acid. The unetched part is coated with wax so that it is protected from the acid. The etched design has a frosted appearance to it because the acid has eaten away a part of the surface. These etches photograph better than cuttings because the design does not reflect the light, but absorbs enough to make the design stand out.

A cutting is done by a wheel. A part of the surface is actually cut away from the glass so that a part of the surface is missing. When the stem itself is cut, it creates some difficulty in identification because some of the original shape is cut away. Light reflects in these cuts making designs somewhat obscure. Etching is a surface application, but cutting goes below the surface.

Hopefully, that will suffice to help you understand the difference enough to know which section to look in; but if not, look in both!

In the back of the book starting on page 154, I have included a sample stem identification from Cambridge, Fostoria, and Tiffin. Also included is an identification page of Cambridge nudes that seem to confuse many collectors and dealers alike.

Prices in this book are only for the cordials, brandies, or pousse-cafes shown. I have even priced the unidentified ones based upon what I was willing to pay for them. You have to use your own judgment on those. Experts in Cambridge, Fostoria, Heisey, and Morgantown have helped me by giving me their ideas as to pricing those company's cordials; but ultimately, I made the final pricing decision.

Let me know if you have suggestions or ideas for any subsequent books. I already know I would use other stems besides cordials because the photography would be simpler. Until then, Happy Hunting!

Why This Book (how it came to be)

It started with frustration — mine. Every time I have tried to identify a stem over the twenty-five years that I have been working with glass, I have had to search through book after book to identify the piece. Often, I could not find the stem in any of my books, but I would have wasted two or three hours of my time searching company by company. I wondered why there wasn't one book that incorporated all major glass companies! That was the germ of an idea that became this book.

Over the years my wife has suggested several times that I do a book on cordials. In fact, the very first cordial collection I bought was purchased with that possibilty in the back of my mind for "someday." Yet, I kept shrugging the idea aside, saying too many of what I had were unidentified. She contended that even unknowns could be given some documentary status by photographing them and putting them before the public in a book. John Q. Public could then identify their stems as the same ones in the book. That's "documentation" of a sort. Further, she felt collectors "in the know" would be willing to contribute their specific knowledge to the body of research if I'd give them the opportunity. Her arguments made sense and gradually made me less uncomfortable about including unknown stems in a book. I actually found myself considering the project!

Once started, the undertaking seemed difficult at best. It turned out to be a monumental project, both from the standpoint of coordination and photography. Luckily, I have been garnering cordials for over twenty years, so I had an assortment of stems for my first attempt to organize such a book. After months of discussing options with Collector Books, we took some test shots in October, 1994. After seeing like cordials (one company or one pattern) grouped together, I felt that there had to be a better idea. One problem was that by photographing six or eight together, no other stem could later be inserted between those already pictured. New stems are always turning up, and I wanted a book that could be added to and expanded over time.

I suggested individual shots of the stems; but then the cost factor reared its ugly head. Months passed and individual photos finally won out. You can thank Collector Books for going out on the cost limb here. That seemed to make everything simple; but, oh was I *wrong!*

Originally we started with 876 cordials that were whittled to 648 for the book due to duplications of stems with four or five different colors. I have quite a few for-eign made cordials that I chose not to include in this book. The first time all my cordials were unpacked and displayed at one time was on six 8' tables at the photography session last October. Dick and Pat Spencer were amazed to see so many. I had told Dick I had over 800 but he said seeing them was still mind boggling! Charley Lynch, photographer, was also overwhelmed! Right now, he doesn't have a fondness for anything that looks like a cordial. Unfortunately, he had to shoot these without help and little knowledge of what part of the design I wanted to show, causing some reshoots as I worked on the book. I've considered starting him on a cordial collection for Christmas this year!

The task of labeling each cordial with a reference number seemed innocent enough until it came time to photograph. We needed removable labels, but some way for the number to show in the photograph and not interfere with the book's layout. Cathy found a children's toy used for teaching counting that seemed to work well. It did when the photographer remembered to change the number to match the cordial's number! Somehow that did not always get done; so there were some extra days sorting out that unforeseen mishap.

Seemingly innocent problems became days of extra work. I originally entered into my computer all of the colors by the glass company's nomenclature. When I went to alphabetize by color, I had Mocha in the M's, Carmen in the C's, and Tahoe in the T's. Since I chose to show the stems by color, I had outfoxed myself. All those company colors had to be re-entered by plain amber, red, and blue. Should there be a next book, I shall be a lot smarter about expanding it!

Billy Schroeder of Collector Books spent a couple of days sorting pictures to match descriptions and colors before I even saw my copies. He did a great job for a novice about glass. Reading my notes must have been a new experience for him, too! I hadn't expected anyone to use those notes but me! Lisa Stroup, editor of Collector Books, worried that no one will ever know all the hours spent on this book because it looks so uncomplicated. Aren't the best books simply done and easy to use? That is what I have always strived for in writing! There are far too many complicated books and instructional guides available without my adding to them!

I hope you enjoy and learn from all our efforts; and I hope we've created a good, quick reference guide for stemware!

Amber

Company	Bryce	Cambridge	Cambridge
Line	946	1066 optic	1341
Pattern	Delhi	Aurora	Mushroom
Color	Amber	Amber	Mocha
Height	3½"	3⅞"	1¹³⁄₁₆"
Price	$18.00	$35.00	$8.00

Company	Cambridge	Cambridge	Cambridge
Line	1402	1402/100	3011/14
Pattern	Tally Ho	Tally Ho	Statuesque
Color	Amber	Amber	Amber
Height	2⅝"	5"	5⅞"
Price	$45.00	$50.00	$400.00

Company	Cambridge	Cambridge	Cambridge
Line	3060	3075	3077
Pattern	703 etch	Imperial Hunt scene	
Color	Amber	Amber gold encrusted	Amber
Height	3¾"	3¾"	3¾"
Price	$50.00	$195.00	$35.00

Stem #2 comes with or without an optic (paneled). Serious collectors try to obtain both types. Stems #4 and #5 are both Tally Ho, but the taller is more expensive and more difficult to find. Cambridge called the treatment on #8 gold encrusted. Concern yourself with making sure this gold is not worn when buying gold decorations.

Amber

Company	Cambridge	Cambridge	Cambridge
Line	3121	3130	3575
Pattern	Portia	Apple Blossom	Stradivari/Regency
Color	Amber	Amber	Amber
Height	4⅞"	4⅜"	5⅜"
Price	$225.00	$100.00	$40.00

Company	Cambridge	Cambridge	Cambridge
Line	3575	7966	7966
Pattern	Stradivari/Regency	Trumpet	Trumpet
Color	Mocha	Amber	Amber foot
Height	5⅜"	4⅞"	4⅞"
Price	$45.00	$25.00	$20.00

Company	Cambridge	Fostoria	Fostoria
Line	3105	5082	5082
Pattern	Rose Point Pressed	Loop Optic	Loop Optic
Color	Amber	Amber/irridized	Amber
Height	4⅝"	3⅝"	3⅝"
Price	$150.00	$30.00	$25.00

Differences in Cambridge's amber are shown by #3 and #4. Mocha was a later color. Pressed Rose Point illustrated by #7 has the pattern moulded into the foot with the top being plain. Stem #8 would have fit in the iridized section but it was placed here to show how the same cordial was sometimes embellished to form another stem line.

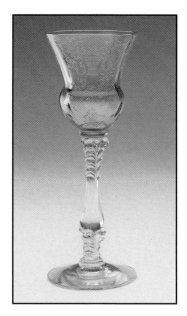

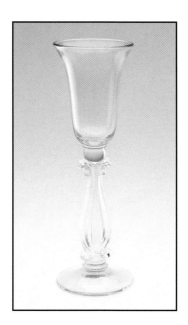

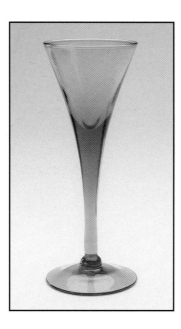

Amber

Company	Fostoria	Fostoria	Fostoria
Line	5093	5097	870
Pattern	Vesper etch 275	Beverly etch 276	Seville etch 274
Color	Amber	Amber	Amber
Height	3⅝"	3⁷⁄₁₆"	3½"
Price	$75.00	$45.00	$65.00

Company	Fry	Heisey	Imperial
Line		3380	
Pattern	Swirl Connector	Empress 447	Pillar Flutes
Color	Amber	Marigold	Amber
Height	2¾"	3¹³⁄₁₆"	3³⁄₁₆"
Price	$35.00	$100.00	$35.00

Company	McKee	New Martinsville	New Martinsville
Line			
Pattern	Rock Crystal	Moondrops	Moondrops
Color	Amber	Amber	Amber w/platinum
Height	2⅞"	3"	3"
Price	$30.00	$25.00	$28.00

Heisey's Marigold color is illustrated by #5. This is the only cordial in this color I have been able to find! Platinum decorations (#9) are usually bypassed if worn.

Amber

Company	New Martinsville	Paden City	Seneca
Line		991	903
Pattern	Radiance	Penny Line	Unidentified
Color	Amber w/platinum	Amber	Amber
Height	2⅝"	3⅜"	3½"
Price	$30.00	$15.00	$25.00

Company	Tiffin	Westmoreland	Unidentified
Line	15011		Unidentified
Pattern	Columbine	Waterford	Unidentified
Color	Amber	Amber foot	Amber etch
Height	5"	2¾"	3⅝"
Price	$40.00	$25.00	$20.00

Company	Unidentified	Unidentified	Unidentified
Line	Unidentified	Unidentified	Unidentified
Pattern	Unidentified	Unidentified	Unidentified
Color	Amber	Amber	Amber/cut top
Height	3⅜"	3¼"	3½"
Price	$18.00	$15.00	$20.00

Four unidentified cordials are pictured here. If you know what any of these stems are, please let me know! I am sure someone will recognize one of these.

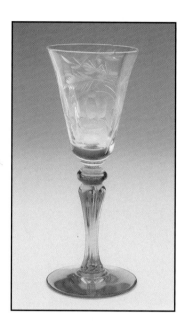

Amethyst

Company	Cambridge	Cambridge	Cambridge
Line	1066 no optic	1327	1341
Pattern	Aurora pousse-cafe		Mushroom
Color	Amethyst	Amethyst light	Amethyst
Height	3⁹⁄₁₆"	3⁵⁄₁₆"	1¹³⁄₁₆"
Price	$40.00	$18.00	$10.00

Company	Cambridge	Cambridge	Cambridge
Line	3011/14	3035	3126
Pattern	Statuesque		
Color	Amethyst	Amethyst	Amethyst
Height	5⅞"	4¹⁵⁄₁₆"	4¹⁵⁄₁₆"
Price	$400.00	$50.00	$60.00

Company	Cambridge	Cambridge	Fostoria
Line	3575	7966	5056
Pattern	Stradivari/Regency	Trumpet	American Lady
Color	Amethyst	Amethyst	Amethyst
Height	5⅜"	4⅞"	3⅛"
Price	$40.00	$25.00	$30.00

Stem #1, a pousse-cafe, seems to be harder to find than a true cordial. Most cordial collectors will buy these as well as brandies for their collections.

Amethyst and Bi-Color

Company	Fostoria	New Martinsville	Unidentified
Line	6011		Unidentified
Pattern	Neo Classic	Moondrops	Unidentified
Color	Amethyst	Amethyst	Amethyst
Height	3³⁄₁₆"	3"	4¾"
Price	$40.00	$28.00	$20.00

Company	Cambridge	Cambridge	Heisey
Line	3035	3085	3350 Wabash
Pattern	Apple Blossom	Peach Blo/Emerald ft.	
Color	Amber/gold krystol		Blue/yellow flashed
Height	4⅞"	3"	3⅞"
Price	$165.00	$65.00	$55.00

Company	Heisey	Heisey	Morgantown
Line	3394	3368 Albermarle	7577
Pattern	Saxony		Venus
Color	Blue/yellow flashed	Yellow/lilac flashed	AnnaRose/Aquamarine
Height	2½"	3½"	3⅞"
Price	$ 50.00	$60.00	$55.00

Stems #6, #7, and #8 show Heisey cordials that were discovered among a large collection of flashed glassware in New England in the late 1970s. This collection contained glass of all major companies with many different treatments on the glass. Some Heisey purists scoff at these pieces because they were not factory adorned. Actually, they look better in a collection than plain crystal!

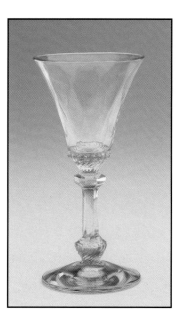

Bi-Color, Tri-Color, and Black

Company	Unidentified	Unidentified	Unidentified
Line	Unidentified	Unidentified	Unidentified
Pattern	Unidentified	Unidentified	Unidentified
Color	Amber/green	Amber/green	Gold/green
Height	5⅛"	3⅛"	4⁷⁄₁₆"
Price	$20.00	$20.00	$25.00

Company	Unidentified	Tiffin	Unidentified
Line	Unidentified	Unidentified	Unidentified
Pattern	Unidentified	Unidentified	Swirled
Color	Pink/aqua	Pink/green	Red/blue/green
Height	3½"	4¾"	3½"
Price	$20.00	$35.00	$15.00

Company	Tiffin	Unidentified	Cambridge
Line	200-1	Unidentified	1327
Pattern	Unidentified	Unidentified	
Color	Yellow/amber	Yellow/amber	Ebony
Height	3⅞"	3⁹⁄₁₆"	3⁵⁄₁₆"
Price	$20.00	$20.00	$30.00

Stem #5 has been identified by several sources as Tiffin, but I found no documentation. Stem #6 is one that I bought just for the color; but, who made it?

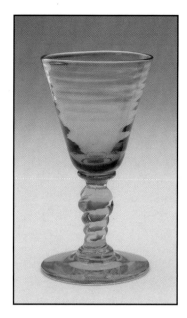

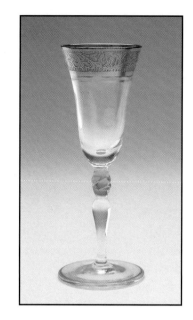

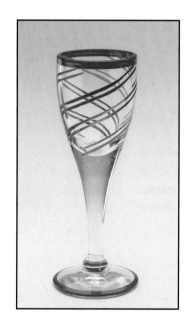

Black and Blue

Company	Imperial	Libbey	Morgantown
Line		Silhouette	7640 Art Moderne
Pattern	Cape Cod	Greyhound	
Color	Black	Black	Ebony stem
Height	3½"	4"	4¾"
Price	$45.00	$200.00	$75.00

Company	Morgantown	Morgantown	Morgantown
Line	7640 Art Moderne	7640 Art Moderne	781
Pattern	Artic 4569	727 Victoria	Fontinelle
Color	Ebony stem	Ebony stem	Ebony filament
Height	4¾"	4¾"	4¼"
Price	$125.00	$85.00	$155.00

Company	Unidentified	Bryce	Cambridge
Line	Unidentified	943	1066 optic
Pattern	Unidentified	Colonade	Aurora
Color	Black stem	Blue	Moonlight blue
Height	3½"	4⅜"	3⅞"
Price	$20.00	$45.00	$45.00

The Cape Cod cigarette lighter (#1) was an attempt to market cordials in another way. Whatever works! Art Deco collectors seek #3, #4, and #5, so there is extra competition for these. Careful! The open stem makes for easier breakage.

Blue

Company	Cambridge	Cambridge	Cambridge
Line	1341	1327	1327
Pattern	Mushroom		
Color	Bluebell	Royal blue	Tahoe blue
Height	1¾"	3⁵⁄₁₆"	3⁵⁄₁₆"
Price	$20.00	$25.00	$25.00

Company	Cambridge	Cambridge	Cambridge
Line	1341	1401	1402
Pattern	Mushroom	Jefferson	Tally Ho
Color	Moonlight blue	Royal blue	Royal blue
Height	1¹³⁄₁₆"	3"	2⅝"
Price	$15.00	$60.00	$60.00

Company	Cambridge	Cambridge	Cambridge
Line	1402/100	300	3011/14
Pattern	Tally Ho	Caprice	Statuesque
Color	Royal blue	Moonlight blue	Royal blue
Height	5"	4⅜"	5⅞"
Price	$65.00	$130.00	$495.00

There are five shades of Cambridge blue shown here with an additional one pictured on page 27 (#1). In collecting cordials, I always look for color as my first criterion. Stem #9 is one of the more desirable Cambridge blue cordials, which also translates into the most expensive blue one.

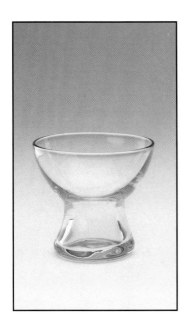

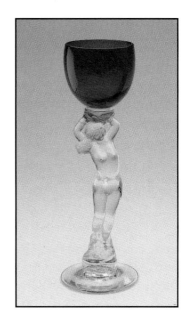

Blue

Company	Cambridge	Cambridge	Cambridge
Line	3077	3077	3077
Pattern	Cleo		
Color	Willow blue	Willow blue	Royal blue
Height	3¾"	3¾"	3¾"
Price	$165.00	$65.00	$60.00

Company	Cambridge	Cambridge	Cambridge
Line	3101	3103	3103
Pattern	pousse-cafe		pousse-cafe
Color	Royal blue foot	Royal blue	Royal blue
Height	3½"	3⁵⁄₁₆"	3⅝"
Price	$55.00	$60.00	$60.00

Company	Cambridge	Cambridge	Cambridge
Line	3112	3122	3130
Pattern			
Color	Royal blue	Royal blue	Willow blue
Height	3⅜"	4¹⁵⁄₁₆"	4⅜"
Price	$75.00	$65.00	$65.00

Stems #2 and #3 show #3077 stemware that is frequently collected for use with the Cambridge Decagon pattern. That stem is most often found etched with Cleo as shown by #1. Stems #5 and #6 show the difference in the #3103 cordial and pousse-cafe. I always try to get one of each when possible.

 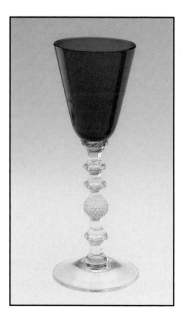 

Blue

Company	Cambridge	Cambridge	Cambridge
Line	3135	3575	3575
Pattern		Stradivari/Regency	Stradivari/Regency
Color	Willow blue	Moonlight blue	Tahoe blue
Height	4½"	5⅜"	5⅜"
Price	$65.00	$60.00	$60.00

Company	West Virginia Specialty	Cambridge	Duncan and Miller Co.
Line		3105	
Pattern	Unidentified	Rose Point Pressed	Carribean
Color	Blue splatter	Royal blue	Blue
Height	4¹⁄₁₆"	3⅝"	3¹⁄₁₆"
Price	20.00	$175.00	$175.00

Company	Duncan & Miller	Fostoria	Fostoria
Line	50	5099	5056
Pattern	Arliss	Kashmir etch 283	American Lady
Color	Cobalt blue	Azure	Royal blue
Height	3¼"	3⅞"	3⅛"
Price	$40.00	$110.00	$35.00

Stem #4 intrigues collectors. It was bought as a Cambridge #7966, but turned out to be a West Virginia Speciality Company cordial. Note that Cambridge #7966 are 4⅞" and have a different stem connection. See #5 and #6 on page 11 for the minor differences. I thought I would find a blue Cambridge #7966 to set beside this one, but it never worked out.

 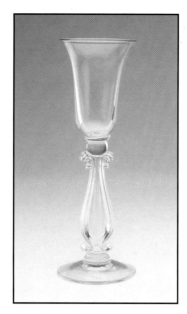 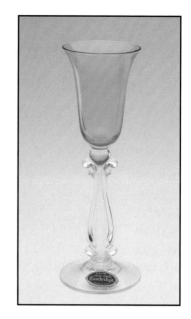

Blue

Company	Fostoria	Fostoria	Fostoria
Line	5082	5098	5098
Pattern	Loop Optic	Versailles etch 278	June etch 279
Color	Azure	Azure	Azure
Height	3¹¹⁄₁₆"	3¹⁵⁄₁₆"	3¹⁵⁄₁₆"
Price	$35.00	$110.00	$150.00

Company	Fostoria	Fostoria	Heisey
Line	6011	6011	3368 Albermarle
Pattern	Neo Classic	Neo Classic brandy	
Color	Royal blue	Royal blue	Blue flashed
Height	3³⁄₁₆"	3¹⁵⁄₁₆"	3½"
Price	$45.00	$45.00	$60.00

Company	Heisey	Heisey	Heisey
Line	3390	3404 Spanish	3416 Barbara Fritchie
Pattern	Carcassone		
Color	Cobalt blue	Cobalt blue	Cobalt blue
Height	2¾"	4¾"	6"
Price	$225.00	$250.00	$390.00

Stems #4 and #5 show the difference in Fostoria's cordial and brandy in the #6011 line. A problem occurs if you have one #6011 and do not know which one you have! Carry an updated list of what you have! I didn't at first and had many duplicates! Doing this book forced me to make an inventory!

Blue

Company	Imperial	Morgantown	Morgantown (?)
Line	56		Twist stem
Pattern	Provencial Blown		Tulip Optic
Color	Turquoise blue	Bristol blue	Aquamarine stem
Height	3⅜"	3"	5⁷⁄₁₆"
Price	$30.00	$30.00	$100.00

Company	Morgantown	Morgantown	Morgantown
Line	7616½ Wescott	7630 Ballerina	7643
Pattern		Sunrise Medallion 758	Golf Ball
Color	Ritz blue filament	Aquamarine	Ritz blue
Height	3⅝"	5⅛"	3⁷⁄₁₆"
Price	$55.00	$250.00	$50.00

Company	Morgantown	Morgantown	Morgantown
Line	7643	7643	7643
Pattern	Golf Ball	Golf Ball	Golf Ball
Color	Aquamarine	Copen blue	Azure stem
Height	3⁷⁄₁₆"	3⁷⁄₁₆"	3½"
Price	$30.00	$30.00	$60.00

Stem #1 is most often confused with a French-made stem that measures the same height. I have a French one labeled P.V. France. The only difference I have been able to verify is in the base diameter. The French is 1¾" while the Imperial is only 1⅝". This is true for the cordial only! Stem #3 is questionable as to being Morgantown; it was definitely Morgantown when I traded for it, but, now....

Blue

Company	Morgantown	Morgantown	Morgantown
Line	7673 Lexington	7725/2	8445
Pattern	Palm Optic bowl	Pagoda	Plantation
Color	Ritz blue filament	Gloria blue	Ritz blue
Height	4¹⁵⁄₁₆"	3¹⁵⁄₁₆"	4⁷⁄₁₆"
Price	$75.00	$65.00	$95.00

Company	Morgantown	Morgantown	Morgantown
Line			
Pattern	Hex	Hex	Hex
Color	Ritz blue filament	Ritz blue filament	Ritz blue filament
Height	3⅜"	3⅞"	4½"
Price	$50.00	$50.00	$55.00

Company	New Martinsville	New Martinsville	New Martinsville
Line			
Pattern	No. 38	Radiance	Moondrops
Color	Cobalt blue	Cobalt blue	Cobalt blue
Height	2⅞"	2⅝"	4"
Price	$30.00	$40.00	$30.00

I bought #3 as Imperial, but it is documented as Morgantown. Thirty Plantation stems were in an antique mall in Florida for over four years with an enormous price on them. I finally negotiated a better price; but the owner only valued them as old "cobalt blue."

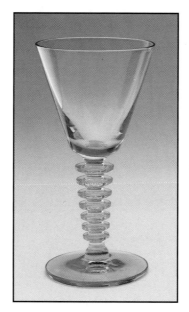

Blue

Company	New Martinsville	Paden City	Seneca
Line		991	Unidentified
Pattern	Radiance	Penny Line	"Baubles"
Color	Blue Light	Cobalt blue	Cobalt blue
Height	2⅝"	3⅜"	4¹⁵⁄₁₆"
Price	$40.00	$20.00	$40.00

Company	Steuben	Tiffin	Tiffin
Line		6776 cordial	6776 sherry
Pattern	Threading	Nude stem	Nude stem
Color	Blue	Cobalt blue frosted	Cobalt blue frosted
Height	4⅜"	5⅛"	5¾"
Price	$175.00	$200.00	$175.00

Company	Unidentified	Unidentified	Unidentified
Line			Unidentified
Pattern	Rooster head	Rooster head	Courting couple
Color	Blue	Blue light	Cobalt blue/gold
Height	3⅜"	3⅜"	3⅝"
Price	$60.00	$60.00	$25.00

Tiffin nude stems are confusing; #5 and #6 show the distinction between cordial and brandy. The rooster heads #7 and #8 are often identified as Morgantown or Imperial, but I have found nothing documenting who actually made them. Can you? Stem #4 see page 121 #3.

Blue

Company	Unidentified	Unidentified	Unidentified
Line	Unidentified	Unidentified	Unidentified
Pattern	Unidentified	Unidentified	Unidentified
Color	Blue	Cobalt blue	Cobalt blue
Height	3⅜"	4½"	3¾"
Price	$20.00	$25.00	$25.00

Company	Bryce	Unidentified	Unidentified
Line	678	Unidentified	Unidentified
Pattern	Unidentified	Unidentified	Twist stem
Color	Cobalt blue	Cobalt blue	Cobalt blue
Height	5¼"	3⁵⁄₁₆"	4⅜"
Price	$25.00	$20.00	$25.00

Company	Bryce	Unidentified	Unidentified
Line	850	Unidentified	Unidentified
Pattern		Unidentified	Unidentified
Color	Crystal	Cobalt blue	Blue etch
Height	3⅝"	4½"	4¹⁄₁₆"
Price	$30.00	$25.00	$30.00

A couple of these were attributed to Bryce, but I need help on the others. Remember that pricing on unidentified stems in this book is determined by what I was willing to pay! Yes, unidentified stems will sell! Stem #6 may be Fry.

39

Blue and Brown

Company	Bryce	Unidentified	Utility Glassworks
Line	935	Unidentified	
Pattern	J—	Unidentified	Cambodia ware
Color	Blue	Blue	Blue light
Height	4⁵⁄₁₆"	3¾"	3⅝"
Price	$25.00	$20.00	$25.00

Company	Morgantown	Unidentified	Unidentified
Line	7643	Unidentified	
Pattern	Golf Ball	Unidentified	Rooster head
Color	Smoke	Brown	Brown
Height	3⁷⁄₁₆"	5⅛"	3⅜"
Price	$25.00	$12.00	$55.00

Company	Unidentified	Unidentified	Unidentified
Line	Unidentified	Unidentified	Unidentified
Pattern	Unidentified	Swirled stem	Crisscross stem
Color	Brown	Brown bowl	Brown bowl
Height	3⁹⁄₁₆"	6¼"	5⅜"
Price	$10.00	$15.00	$20.00

Stem #1 was found in a 1916 catalog shared with me by Replacements, Inc.; unfortunately, the name was obliterated in the copy so that all I know is that the name starts with the letter J. The color brown is not a prevalent stem line color today, but was earlier this century.

Crystal

Company	Anchor Hocking	Bryce	Bryce
Line		791	943
Pattern	Colonial	Ringmont	Colonade
Color	Crystal	Crystal	Crystal
Height	3^{11}/$_{16}$"	4^3/$_8$"	4^5/$_{16}$"
Price	$20.00	$12.00	$25.00

Company	Bryce	Cambridge	Cambridge
Line	Unidentified		1402/100
Pattern	Ingrid	Mt. Vernon	Tally Ho
Color	Crystal	Crystal	Crystal
Height	3^{11}/$_{16}$"	2^3/$_4$"	5"
Price	$12.00	$22.00	$50.00

Company	Cambridge	Cambridge	Cambridge
Line	1936	1937	1953
Pattern	Pristine tall stem	Pristine short stem	Cathedral
Color	Crystal	Crystal	Crystal
Height	4^3/$_8$"	3^5/$_{16}$	3^1/$_2$"
Price	$35.00	$35.00	$20.00

Several different companies made a stem line similar to #4.

 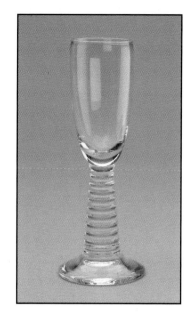 

Crystal

Company	Cambridge	Cambridge	Cambridge
Line	1957	2800	300
Pattern	Sonata	Colonial type	Caprice
Color	Crystal	Crystal	Crystal
Height	3⁹⁄₁₆"	3⅞"	4⅜"
Price	$35.00	$30.00	$42.00

Company	Cambridge	Cambridge	Cambridge
Line	301	3011/14	3103
Pattern	Caprice	Statuesque	
Color	Crystal	Crystal	Crystal
Height	3⅝"	5⅞"	3⁵⁄₁₆"
Price	$45.00	$400.00	$35.00

Company	Cambridge	Cambridge	Cambridge
Line	3114	3121	3126
Pattern		Brandy	
Color	Crystal	Crystal	Crystal
Height	5⅛"	4"	4⅞"
Price	$35.00	$40.00	$35.00

Stem #1 has an original company inventory sticker. Stem #5 is the rarest of the Cambridge Statuesque cordials.

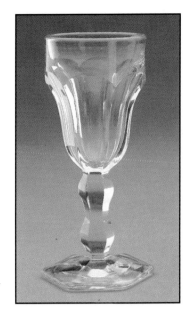

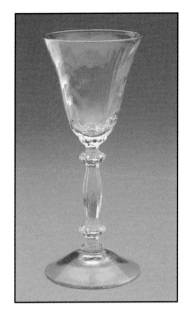

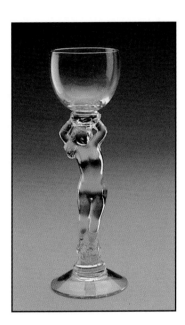

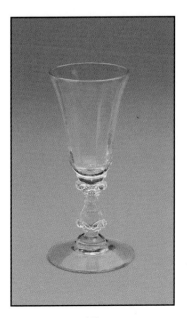

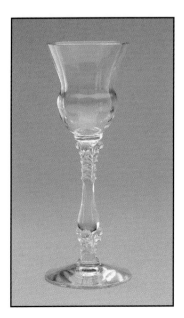

Crystal

Company	Cambridge	Cambridge	Cambridge
Line	3500	3775	3575
Pattern	Gadroon	Arlington	Stradivari/Regency
Color	Crystal	Crystal	Crystal
Height	5"	4¾"	5⅜"
Price	$35.00	$45.00	$40.00

Company	Cambridge	Cambridge	Cambridge
Line	3776	3795	3797
Pattern	Shelburne	Allegro	Square
Color	Crystal	Crystal	Crystal
Height	4⅜"	3¾"	2⅛"
Price	$40.00	$40.00	$20.00

Company	Cambridge	Cambridge	Central
Line	7967		1470 factory label
Pattern	Melody	Rose Point Pressed	10 Optic
Color	Crystal	Crystal	Crystal
Height	3⁵⁄₁₆"	4⅝"	4⅝"
Price	$40.00	$150.00	$50.00

Stem #9 has a factory label identifying it. This is the same stem that Imperial used for one of their Cambridge etchings (Wildflower) when they incorporated Cambridge patterns into their line after the Cambridge plant closure in the mid 1950s.

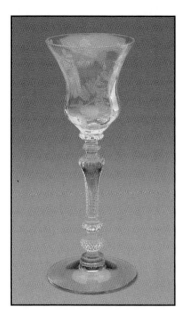

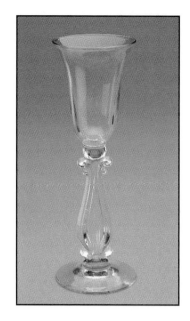

47

Crystal

Company	Duncan & Miller	Duncan & Miller	Duncan & Miller
Line		D-4	No. 503
Pattern	Carribean	Lily of the Valley	Touraine
Color	Crystal	Crystal	Crystal
Height	3¹⁄₁₆"	5"	3⅜"
Price	$65.00	$50.00	$25.00

Company	Fostoria	Fostoria	Fostoria
Line	5056	5098	6016
Pattern	American Lady	Fairfax	Wilma
Color	Crystal	Crystal	Crystal
Height	3⅛"	3¹⁵⁄₁₆"	3¹⁵⁄₁₆"
Price	$25.00	$25.00	$25.00

Company	Fostoria	Fostoria	Heisey
Line	6024	6052	
Pattern	Cellini	Moon Ring	Plantation
Color	Crystal	Crystal	Crystal
Height	3¾"	3⅛"	3⅜"
Price	$25.00	$30.00	$150.00

Most of Fostoria's stem lines were given a name; many companies had only a number for their lines. Stem #6 is the blank (Wilma) more often seen etched with Navarre or Meadow Rose.

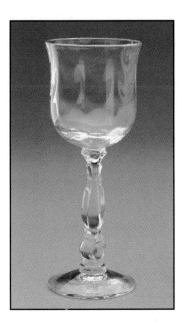

Crystal

Company	Heisey	Heisey	Heisey
Line	5th Avenue		1000
Pattern	Colonial #347	Greek Key	Carlsbad
Color	Crystal	Crystal	Crystal
Height	3¼"	3"	3½"
Price	$30.00	$250.00	$70.00

Company	Heisey	Heisey	Heisey
Line	300	3350 Wabash	3357 King Arthur
Pattern	Peerless		
Color	Crystal	Crystal	Crystal
Height	3⁵⁄₁₆"	3⅞"	6⅝"
Price	$40.00	$45.00	$110.00

Company	Heisey	Heisey	Heisey
Line	3389 Duquense	3404 Spanish	3408 Jamestown
Pattern			
Color	Crystal	Crystal	Crystal
Height	4"	4¾"	4⅜"
Price	$45.00	$40.00	$30.00

Stem #3 is a Heisey pattern that was once thought rare; time has proven that wrong. By the same token, several patterns once thought common place are rarely seen.

 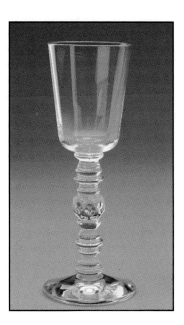 

Crystal

Company	Heisey	Heisey	Heisey
Line	3411 Monte Cristo	3416 Barbara Fritchie	3418
Pattern			Savoy Plaza
Color	Crystal	Crystal	Crystal
Height	5¹³⁄₁₆"	6"	3¾"
Price	$70.00	$100.00	$40.00

Company	Heisey	Heisey	Heisey
Line	363	4044	4083
Pattern	Colonial	New Era	Stanhope
Color	Crystal	Crystal	Crystal
Height	3½"	3½"	3⁹⁄₁₆"
Price	$25.00	$32.00	$50.00

Company	Heisey	Heisey	Heisey
Line	5013 Shasta	5058	5078 Park Avenue
Pattern		Goose	
Color	Crystal	Crystal	Crystal
Height	5¹⁄₁₆"	5¾"	6⅝"
Price	$75.00	$180.00	$100.00

The #2 stem is very fragile at the foot attachment. That fact is one I have learned twice over the years. Deco collectors are very fond of New Era stemware. Although it could never be considered rare, it is quite desirable. Stem #9 is often confused with Libbey stems, but Park Avenue stems are marked Heisey.

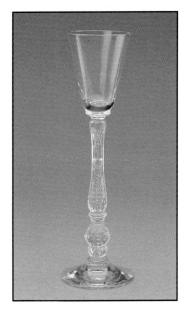

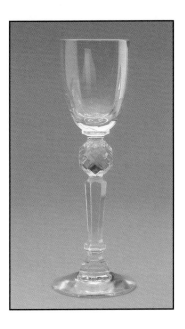
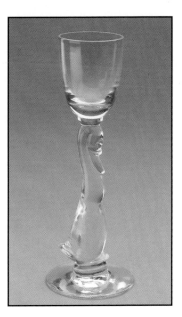

Crystal

Company	Heisey	Heisey	Heisey
Line	5082 Mid Century	5083 El Rancho	6091 Cabochon
Pattern			
Color	Crystal	Crystal	Crystal
Height	4"	5¼"	3½"
Price	$40.00	$75.00	$35.00

Company	Imperial	Imperial	Imperial
Line	3400	3800	400/190
Pattern	Candlewick	Candlewick	Candlewick
Color	Crystal	Crystal	Crystal
Height	4½"	3¼"	4"
Price	$35.00	$45.00	$75.00

Company	Imperial	Libbey	Libbey
Line	400/195	3002	
Pattern	Candlewick brandy		Nob Hill
Color	Crystal	Crystal	Crystal
Height	3⅝"	4³⁄₁₆"	3¹⁵⁄₁₆"
Price	$200.00	$14.00	$6.00

Stem #7 depicts a Candlewick brandy that holds 2 ozs. There is no cordial in this line, so the brandy has to suffice. Stem #9 is often confused with Candlewick.

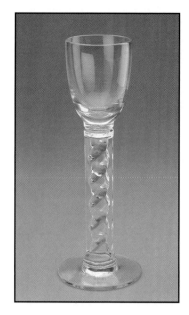
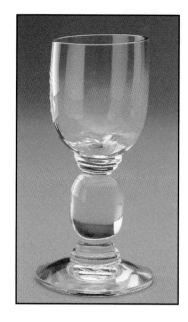

Crystal

Company	Mckee	McKee	Morgantown
Line	Rock crystal	Greek wine	7023
Pattern		Colonial type	Cog base
Color	Crystal	Crystal	Crystal
Height	2⅞"	4³⁄₁₆"	4⅜"
Price	$18.00	$20.00	$35.00

Company	Morgantown	Morgantown	New Martinsville
Line	7037	8446	No. 14
Pattern	Harvard 1 oz. brandy	Summer Cornocopia	"Raindrop"
Color	Crystal	Crystal	Crystal
Height	3⅜"	4⅛"	2¾"
Price	$30.00	$165.00	$25.00

Company	Tiffin	Tiffin	Tiffin
Line	14180	17363	17378 optic
Pattern	Thistle	Paula	
Color	Crystal	Crystal	Crystal
Height	3¹³⁄₁₆"	4"	5⅝"
Price	$30.00	$30.00	$20.00

Stem #5 is another fragile stem. There is little to support the top especially in larger sizes. Stem #6 has been dubbed "Raindrop" by collectors.

  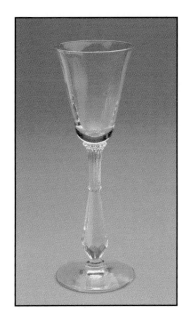

Crystal

Company	Tiffin	Tiffin	Tiffin
Line	17392	17457	17471
Pattern	Encanto		
Color	Crystal	Crystal	Crystal
Height	5⅛"	5⅜"	4⅜"
Price	$25.00	$25.00	$30.00

Company	Tiffin	Tiffin	Westmoreland
Line	17601	17624	
Pattern	Olympia	Beaumont	Thousand Eye
Color	Crystal	Crystal	Crystal
Height	4⅛"	3¼"	3½"
Price	$30.00	$25.00	$20.00

Company	Bryce	Bryce	Fostoria
Line	850	867 Block Optic	6033
Pattern		St. Moritz brandy	Mademoiselle
Color	Crystal	Crystal	Crystal
Height	3½"	4½"	3¹¹⁄₁₆"
Price	$18.00	$20.00	$15.00

The bottom row were all identified after picture placements were made for the book. Sorry!

Crystal Cut

Company	Cambridge	Cambridge	Cambridge
Line	1953	3114	3116
Pattern	Cathedral Silver Wheat	Candlelight cut	Lucia
Color	Crystal cut	Crystal cut	Crystal cut
Height	3½"	5"	5¼"
Price	$60.00	$250.00	$60.00

Company	Cambridge	Cambridge	Cambridge
Line	3120	3134	3139
Pattern	Achilles	Broadmore	Unidentified
Color	Crystal cut	Crystal cut	Crystal cut
Height	4⅞"	4⅝"	4½"
Price	$75.00	$75.00	$45.00

Company	Cambridge	Cambridge	Cambridge
Line	3500	3700	3725
Pattern	Adonis	Ardsley	Radiant Rose
Color	Crystal cut	Crystal cut	Crystal cut
Height	5"	4½"	4½"
Price	$65.00	$40.00	$60.00

Crystal cut cordials are the most difficult to identify. When stems were cut, all points of reference were destroyed. Stem #2 took me months to decide to pay the price!

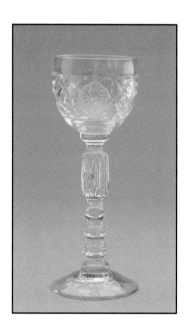

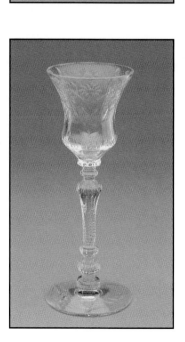

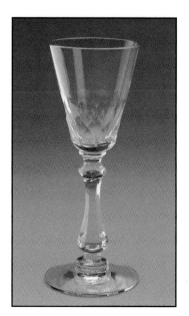

Crystal Cut

Company	Cambridge	Cambridge	Cambridge
Line	3700	3700	3750
Pattern	King Edward	Manor	Euclid
Color	Crystal cut	Crystal cut	Crystal cut
Height	4½"	4½"	4⅜"
Price	$45.00	$40.00	$40.00

Company	Cambridge	Cambridge	Cambridge
Line	3750	3750	3750
Pattern	Ivy	Harvest	Unknown cut
Color	Crystal cut	Crystal cut	Crystal cut
Height	4⅜"	4⅜"	4⅜"
Price	$60.00	$50.00	$40.00

Company	Cambridge	Cambridge	Cambridge
Line	3750	3776	3776
Pattern	Minton Wreath	Maryland	Unknown cut
Color	Crystal cut	Crystal cut	Crystal cut
Height	4¼"	4⅜"	4⅜"
Price	$50.00	$50.00	$40.00

Stems #6 and #9 are both Cambridge stems, but I have been unable to determine the cutting on them!

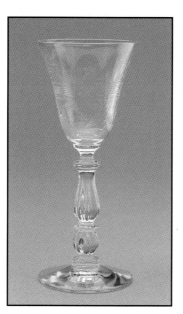

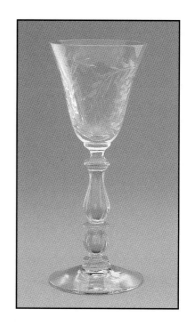

63

Crystal Cut

Company	Cambridge	Cambridge	Cambridge
Line	3795	7801	7966
Pattern	Allegro w/cut	Star cut	Lexington
Color	Crystal cut	Crystal cut	Crystal cut
Height	3¹³⁄₁₆"	4¹⁄₁₆"	4⅞"
Price	$50.00	$35.00	$40.00

Company	Cambridge	Cambridge	Cambridge
Line	7966	7966	a56 Today
Pattern	Laurel Wreath	Wedding Rings	Tomorrow
Color	Crystal cut	Crystal cut	Crystal cut
Height	4⅞"	4⅞"	3⅞"
Price	$40.00	$40.00	$45.00

Company	Duncan and Miller Co.	Duncan and Miller Co.	Duncan and Miller Co.
Line	Canterbury	Canterbury	DC-4
Pattern	Tristine	Phoebus	Lily of the Valley
Color	Crystal cut	Crystal cut	Crystal cut
Height	4¼"	4¼"	5"
Price	$80.00	$70.00	$75.00

Stem #1 is a Cambridge cut. Stem #5 is a pleasing pattern that should have captured more consumers from its Wedding Rings name than it obviously did judging by the lack of those stems found today. Stem #6 is an a56 Today stem with the Tomorrow pattern. Who thought that one up? Stem #9 has a Lily of the Valley stem with a cutting of the same pattern on the bowl.

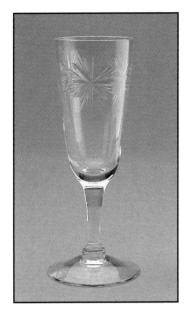

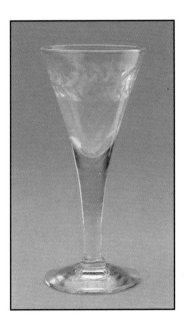

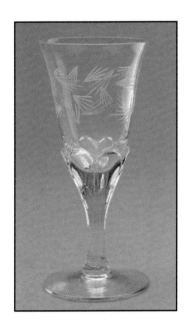

65

Crystal Cut

Company	Duncan & Miller	Duncan & Miller	Duncan & Miller
Line	504 Granada	D-2	D-8
Pattern	Alhambra cut 607	Mesa	Starlight
Color	Crystal cut	Crystal cut	Crystal cut
Height	4"	3⅞"	5"
Price	$55.00	$54.00	$50.00

Company	Duncan & Miller	Fostoria	Fostoria
Line	No. 22	4024 Star cut	6030
Pattern	Astaire	Victorian Lady	Holly cut 815
Color	Crystal cut	Crystal cut	Crystal cut
Height	3¼"	3"	3¹³⁄₁₆"
Price	$50.00	$25.00	$30.00

Company	Fostoria	Glastonbury Lotus	Heisey
Line	6030	7695	3366 Trojan
Pattern	Trellis cut 822	F Star cut #32	Hawkes cut
Color	Crystal cut	Crystal cut	Crystal cut
Height	3¹³⁄₁₆"	4"	3¼"
Price	$30.00	$30.00	$50.00

Stem #3 is a D-8 Duncan stem which is a personal favorite of mine. Stem #9 is a Hawkes cutting on a Heisey stem. Can you document the cutting?

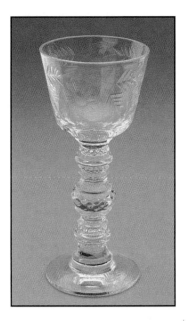

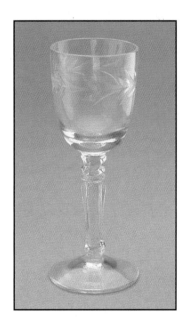

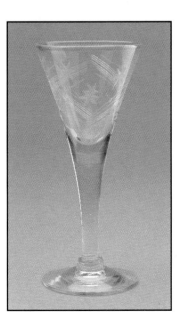

Crystal Cut

Company	Heisey	Heisey	Heisey
Line	3389 Duquense	3404 Spanish	3404 Spanish
Pattern	Monogrammed CSG	Pairpoint cutting	
Color	Crystal cut	Crystal cut	Crystal cut
Height	4"	4¾"	4¾"
Price	$25.00	$75.00	$60.00

Company	Heisey	Heisey	Heisey
Line	3404 Spanish	3408 Jamestown	3411 Monte Cristo
Pattern		Barcelona	Kalarma
Color	Crystal cut	Crystal cut	Crystal cut
Height	4¾"	4⅜"	4¾"
Price	$60.00	$60.00	$130.00

Company	Heisey	Heisey	Heisey
Line	3416 Barabara Fritchie	4044 New Era	5010 Symphone
Pattern	Manhattan	Venus	Danish Princes 921
Color	Crystal cut	Crystal cut	Crystal cut
Height	6"	3½"	5⅜"
Price	$110.00	$50.00	$120.00

The monogram on #1 lessens the value unless you can find a CSG who wants to own it. Stem #2 is a Pairpoint cutting on a Heisey Spanish stem. Stems #3 and #4 are unidentified cuttings on Spanish stems. They may be Heisey or could be some other company's cuttings.

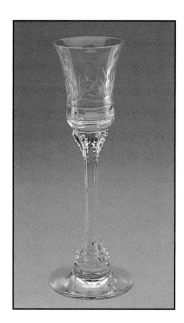

Crystal Cut

Company	Heisey	Heisey	Heisey
Line	5022 Graceful	5024 Oxford	5024 Oxford
Pattern	942 Harvester	Ivy	Victoria cut 1086
Color	Crystal cut	Crystal cut	Crystal cut
Height	4¾"	4⁹⁄₁₆"	4⁹⁄₁₆"
Price	$65.00	$40.00	$40.00

Company	Heisey	Heisey	Heisey
Line	5057 Suez	5089 Princess	6091 Cabochon
Pattern	Unidentified	Nonchalance 1076	Unidentified
Color	Crystal cut	Crystal cut	Crystal cut
Height	4⁹⁄₁₆"	4⁹⁄₁₆"	3½"
Price	$35.00	$60.00	$45.00

Company	Heisey	Heisey	Imperial
Line	6091 Cabochon	Lariat	3400 Star cut
Pattern	Debutante	Moonglo	Candlewick
Color	Crystal cut	Crystal cut	Crystal cut
Height	3⁷⁄₁₆"	4⁹⁄₁₆"	4½"
Price	$55.00	$135.00	$50.00

All of the cuts on this page are documented Heisey cuttings except for #4 and #6 that I have been unable to verify the cut pattern.

Crystal Cut

Company	Libbey Rock Sharpe	Libbey Rock Sharpe	Libbey Rock Sharpe
Line	1008	1008-2	1013
Pattern	Buckingham cut 1008	Cut 1008	Unidentified
Color	Crystal cut	Crystal cut	Crystal cut
Height	5½"	5½"	4½"
Price	$30.00	$30.00	$25.00

Company	Libbey Rock Sharpe	Libbey Rock Sharpe	Libbey Rock Sharpe
Line	1016-1	1017	2010
Pattern	Cut 1016	Burma	Unidentified
Color	Crystal cut	Crystal cut	Crystal cut
Height	4⅝"	4⁷⁄₁₆"	4¼"
Price	$35.00	$30.00	$25.00

Company	Libbey Rock Sharpe	Morgantown (?)	Morgantown
Line	3005	Twist stem	7643
Pattern	Arctic Rose aka "Dover"	"Little Bo-Peep"	Golf Ball
Color	Crystal cut	Crystal cut	Crystal cut
Height	4¹¹⁄₁₆"	4"	3⁷⁄₁₆"
Price	$20.00	$100.00	$25.00

Stems #1 – #7 are Libbey Rock Sharpe stems, but the pattern names are still mostly elusive. Stem #7 was widely distributed. Stem #8 was represented to be Morgantown, but documentation has not been forthcoming.

Crystal Cut

Company	New Martinsville	Tiffin	Tiffin
Line		15074	17301
Pattern	Moondrops	Unidentified	Athlone
Color	Crystal cut	Crystal cut	Crystal cut
Height	3"	5½"	4¼"
Price	$20.00	$30.00	$35.00

Company	Tiffin	Tiffin	Tiffin
Line	17361	17365	17372
Pattern	Adoration	Cascade	Parkwood
Color	Crystal cut	Crystal cut	Crystal cut
Height	4⁵⁄₁₆"	3⅞"	4⁹⁄₁₆"
Price	$35.00	$25.00	$35.00

Company	Tiffin	Tiffin	Tiffin
Line	17378	17378	17392
Pattern	True Love	Wreath	Kingsley
Color	Crystal cut	Crystal cut	Crystal cut
Height	5⅛"	5⅛"	5⅛"
Price	$35.00	$35.00	$35.00

Tiffin's stemware lines and patterns have been well documented by Replacements, Inc. Their help in identification was invaluable.

 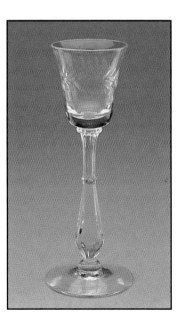 

Crystal Cut

Company	Tiffin	Tiffin	Tiffin
Line	17457	17501	17574
Pattern	Baroque	Carole	Chilton
Color	Crystal cut	Crystal cut	Crystal cut
Height	5⅜"	4¹⁵⁄₁₆"	3¹³⁄₁₆"
Price	$35.00	$30.00	$35.00

Company	Tiffin	Tiffin	Tiffin
Line	17594	17594	17614
Pattern	Sample	Cameo	Dawn
Color	Crystal cut	Crystal cut	Crystal cut
Height	5¼"	5⅜"	4"
Price	$165.00	$35.00	$35.00

Company	Tiffin	Tiffin	Tiffin
Line	17621	17621	17623-1
Pattern	Parkwood	Sylvan	Parkwood
Color	Crystal cut	Crystal etch	Crystal cut
Height	3⅞"	3⅞"	5⅞"
Price	$35.00	$35.00	$35.00

Stem #4 is cut "Sample" on the foot. Evidently this was a salesman's sample or some showroom stem. It is the only sample in my collection!

Crystal Cut

Company	Tiffin	Unidentified	Hawkes
Line	17724	Unidentified	6030
Pattern	Harvest	Unidentified	Chantilly
Color	Crystal cut	Crystal cut	Crystal cut
Height	6⁵⁄₁₆"	4¹⁵⁄₁₆"	4⁷⁄₁₆"
Price	$40.00	$20.00	$85.00

Company	Unidentified	Astral	Unidentified
Line	Unidentified	Unidentified	Unidentified
Pattern	Unidentified	Questa	Unidentified
Color	Crystal cut	Crystal cut	Crystal cut
Height	4"	4⅛"	4⅝"
Price	$12.00	$15.00	$15.00

Company	Unidentified	Unidentified	Huntington
Line	Unidentified	Unidentified	Unidentified
Pattern	Unidentified	Unidentified	Unidentified
Color	Crystal cut	Crystal cut	Crystal cut
Height	4¼"	3⅝"	5⅛"
Price	$25.00	$30.00	$30.00

Originally, all of the cordials on the next three pages were mysteries when the pages for this book were first laid out. Origins of three on this page were since found. Stem #5 was shown in a catalog at Replacements. We know Astra has offices in New York. Other than that...!

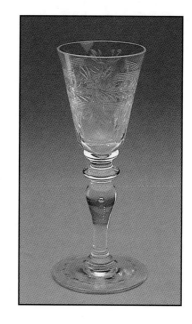

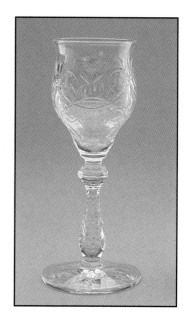

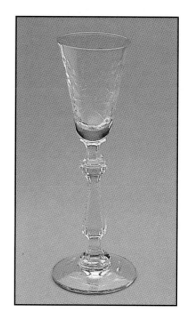

Crystal Cut

	Company	Line	Pattern	Color	Height	Price
	Huntington	Unidentified	Unidentified	Crystal cut	5$\frac{1}{16}$"	$30.00
	Tiffin	15082	Unidentified	Crystal cut	4"	$20.00
	Libbey	2010	Unidentified	Crystal cut	5$\frac{13}{16}$"	$15.00

	Company	Line	Pattern	Color	Height	Price
	Unidentified	Unidentified	Unidentified	Crystal cut	4$\frac{1}{2}$"	$20.00
	Unidentified	Unidentified	Unidentified	Crystal cut	3$\frac{7}{8}$"	$20.00
	Seneca	486	Cut 62	Crystal cut	4$\frac{1}{4}$"	$15.00

	Company	Line	Pattern	Color	Height	Price
	Unidentified	Unidentified	Unidentified	Crystal cut	3$\frac{13}{16}$"	$15.00
	Unidentified	Unidentified	Unidentified	Crystal cut	5"	$15.00
	Hawkes	7330	Wheat	Crystal cut	4$\frac{3}{8}$"	$25.00

Ultimately, I left these stem arrangements alone even though they are out of order alphabetically. Changing one stem meant moving and adjusting all of the pages in the Crystal Cut section, a nightmare!

Crystal Cut

Company	Glastonbury Lotus	Hawkes	Unidentified
Line	67	7240	Unidentified
Pattern	Hostess cut 17	Madison	Unidentified
Color	Crystal cut	Crystal cut	Crystal cut
Height	4⁵⁄₁₆"	5⁵⁄₁₆"	3¼"
Price	$15.00	$25.00	$15.00

Company	Unidentified	Seneca	Unidentified
Line	Unidentified	352	Unidentified
Pattern	Unidentified	Ardis Cut 1262	Unidentified
Color	Crystal cut	Crystal cut	Crystal cut
Height	4¹⁄₁₆"	4"	4"
Price	$20.00	$20.00	$10.00

Company	Unidentified	Unidentified	Tiffin
Line	Unidentified	Unidentified	17361
Pattern	Unidentified	Unidentified	Priscilla
Color	Crystal cut	Crystal cut	Crystal cut
Height	4³⁄₁₆"	3³⁄₁₆"	4³⁄₁₆"
Price	$12.00	$15.00	$25.00

Four mysteries were solved before deadline on this page. That made a total of twelve of the unknown cuts found in the twelfth hour!

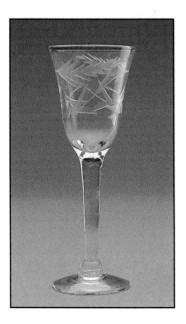

Crystal Etch

Company	Bryce	Cambridge	Cambridge
Line	Unidentified	1066 optic	1327
Pattern	Etch 398	Diane	Elaine
Color	Crystal etch	Crystal etch	Crystal etch
Height	3⅝"	3⅜"	3⁵⁄₁₆"
Price	$15.00	$75.00	$50.00

Company	Cambridge	Cambridge	Cambridge
Line	1327	1936	3106
Pattern	Apple Blossom	Firenze	Rose Point
Color	Crystal etch	Crystal etch	Crystal etch
Height	3⁵⁄₁₆"	4⅜"	4⅞"
Price	$95.00	$50.00	$100.00

Company	Cambridge	Cambridge	Cambridge
Line	3109	3126	3121
Pattern	Vintage	Portia	Rose Point brandy
Color	Crystal etch	Crystal etch	Crystal etch
Height	4"	4⅞"	3¹⁵⁄₁₆"
Price	$45.00	$60.00	$125.00

We were able to identify etchings more easily than cuttings. It may be that I only bought etchings that I knew more than I did cuttings that appealed to me. Stem #5 Firenze appears only on this Cambridge stem unlike most Cambridge etches that appear on several different stems.

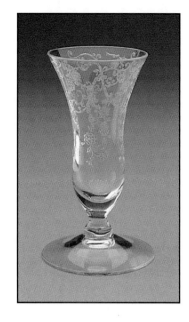

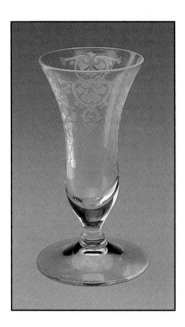
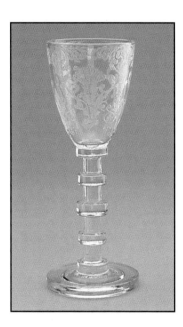

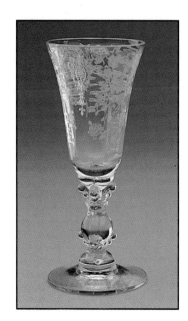

Crystal Etch

Company	Cambridge	Cambridge	Cambridge
Line	3121	3121 optic	3122
Pattern	Rose Point	Elaine	Portia
Color	Crystal etch	Crystal etch	Crystal etch
Height	4⅞"	4¹⁵⁄₁₆"	4¹⁵⁄₁₆"
Price	$70.00	$60.00	$65.00

Company	Cambridge	Cambridge	Cambridge
Line	3122	3130	3120
Pattern	Diane	Portia	Gloria
Color	Crystal etch	Crystal etch	Crystal etch
Height	4⅞"	4¾"	4¹⁵⁄₁₆"
Price	$60.00	$60.00	$75.00

Company	Cambridge	Cambridge	Cambridge
Line	3120	3500	3500
Pattern	Apple Blossom	Elaine	Diane
Color	Crystal etch	Crystal etch	Crystal etch
Height	4¾"	5"	5"
Price	$60.00	$60.00	$75.00

Stem #2 is the only etched #3121 Cambridge stem that I have with an optic (paneled). Optics change the eye's view of a pattern as well as the camera's because of light refraction.

 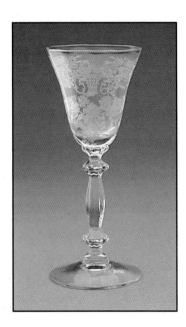 

Crystal Etch

Company	Cambridge	Cambridge	Cambridge
Line	3600	3625 (bowl shape)	3675 (bowl shape)
Pattern	Chantilly	Chantilly	Blossom Time
Color	Crystal etch	Crystal etch	Crystal etch
Height	4¾"	4¾"	5"
Price	$60.00	$60.00	$60.00

Company	Cambridge	Cambridge	Cambridge
Line	37??	3779	3779
Pattern	Wildflower	Chantilly	Daffodil
Color	Crystal etch	Crystal etch	Crystal etch
Height	4½"	4⅜"	4⅜"
Price	$65.00	$60.00	$65.00

Company	Cambridge	Cambridge	Cambridge
Line	3779	3790	7606
Pattern	Roselyn	Magnolia	Marjorie brandy
Color	Crystal etch	Crystal etch	Crystal etch
Height	4⅜"	3½"	3⁵⁄₁₆"
Price	$60.00	$50.00	$100.00

Stems #1 – 3 have the same stem but different line numbers. The shape of the bowl determines what line. Stem #4 is a #3700 Cambridge line, but the exact number is unknown at present.

89

Crystal Etch

Company	Cambridge	Cambridge	Cambridge
Line	7606	7606	7966
Pattern	Marjorie cordial	Marjorie pousse-cafe	Lily of the Valley
Color	Crystal etch	Crystal etch	Crystal etch
Height	3¾"	3⅞"	4⅞"
Price	$100.00	$100.00	$50.00

Company	Cambridge	Central	Central
Line	7966	1470	Unidentified
Pattern	Rose Point	Imperial Wildflower	Harding
Color	Crystal etch	Crystal etch	Crystal etch
Height	4⅞"	4⅝"	4⅛"
Price	$100.00	$100.00	$40.00

Company	Duncan & Miller	Duncan & Miller	Fostoria
Line	5111½	5326	660
Pattern	First Love	Charmaine Rose	Mystic etch 270
Color	Crystal etch	Crystal etch	Crystal etch
Height	3⅝"	5"	3⁹⁄₁₆"
Price	$70.00	$75.00	$35.00

Stems #1 and #2 along with #9 pictured on page 89 show the minor differences in heights of the brandy, cordial, and pousse-cafe of one pattern. You can see why some collectors only seek one of the three sizes. Avid collectors want them all! Stem #5 is a Central stem etched with Cambridge's Wildflower at Imperial. Imperial bought Central's stem, but it makes for some serious confusion. (See #9 on page 47.)

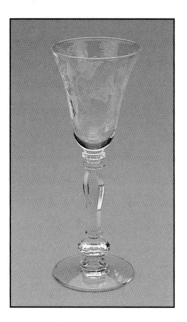

Crystal Etch

Company	Fostoria	Fostoria	Fostoria
Line	660	5098	6009
Pattern	Washington etch 266	June etch 279	Midnight Rose etch 316
Color	Crystal etch	Crystal etch	Crystal etch
Height	3⅝"	3¹⁵⁄₁₆"	3¾"
Price	$35.00	$50.00	$35.00

Company	Fostoria	Fostoria	Fostoria
Line	6016	6016	6020
Pattern	Navarre etch 327	Meadow Rose etch 328	Mayflower etch 332
Color	Crystal etch	Crystal etch	Crystal etch
Height	3¹³⁄₁₆"	3⅞"	3⅞"
Price	$50.00	$50.00	$45.00

Company	Fostoria	Fostoria	Fostoria
Line	6023	6024	6026
Pattern	Willow etch 335	Wilomere etch 333	Chintz etch 338
Color	Crystal etch	Crystal etch	Crystal etch
Height	3¼"	3¾"	3¹⁵⁄₁₆"
Price	$40.00	$40.00	$40.00

Notice that each Fostoria etching has a factory assigned number. Stems #4 and #5 are often confused by novice collectors and dealers. The design etch is more complete on Navarre than the open centered design of Meadow Rose.

Crystal Etch

Company	Fostoria	Fostoria	Glastonbury Lotus
Line	6030	6037	75
Pattern	Buttercup etch 340	Heather etch 343	Vesta etch 104
Color	Crystal etch	Crystal etch	Crystal etch
Height	$3^{13}/_{16}$"	$4^{1}/_{16}$"	4"
Price	$40.00	$40.00	$30.00

Company	Heisey	Heisey	Heisey
Line	3318 Waldorf	3350 Wabash	3366
Pattern	Chateau	Pied Piper	Trojan 445
Color	Crystal etch	Crystal etch	Crystal etch
Height	$3^{7}/_{16}$"	$3^{7}/_{8}$"	$3^{1}/_{4}$"
Price	$95.00	$60.00	$60.00

Company	Heisey	Heisey	Heisey
Line	3368 Albermarle	3389 Duquense	3389 Duquense
Pattern	Trojan	Normandie 35-81	Chintz
Color	Crystal etch	Crystal etch	Crystal etch
Height	$3^{1}/_{2}$"	4"	4"
Price	$55.00	$60.00	$100.00

Stem #4 gave some experienced Heisey collectors research problems! It is a more delicate etch than those normally found on Heisey stems.

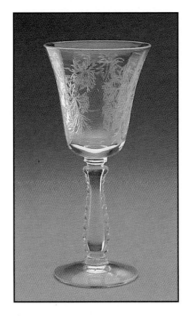

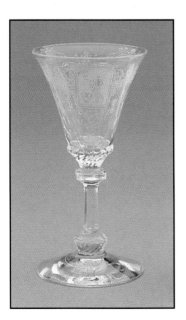

Crystal Etch

Company	Heisey	Heisey	Heisey
Line	4085 Kohinoor	5010 Symphone	5010 Symphone
Pattern	Coronation	Minuet	Crinoline
Color	Crystal etch	Crystal etch	Crystal etch
Height	4"	5⅜"	5⅜"
Price	$60.00	$125.00	$75.00

Company	Heisey	Heisey	Heisey
Line	5072	5089 Princess	5024 Oxford
Pattern	Rose	Orchid	Orchid 1978
Color	Crystal etch	Crystal etch	Crystal etch
Height	4¼"	4⁹⁄₁₆"	4⁷⁄₁₆"
Price	$155.00	$135.00	$15.00

Company	Heisey	Heisey	Heisey
Line	5024 Oxford	5024 Oxford	5024 Oxford
Pattern	Rose 1979	Old Colony 1980	Titania 1981
Color	Crystal etch	Crystal etch	Crystal etch
Height	4⁷⁄₁₆"	4⁷⁄₁₆"	4⁷⁄₁₆"
Price	$15.00	$15.00	$15.00

This page shows some of the most collected Heisey patterns. Starting with #7 and continuing through #2 on page 99 are Oxford stems issued by the Heisey club as a money making project from 1978 to 1983. One stem was made each year.

97

Crystal Etch

Company	Heisey	Heisey	Imperial
Line	5024 Oxford	5024 Oxford	3400 Wild Rose
Pattern	Coronation 1982	Swingtime 1983	Candlewick
Color	Crystal etch	Crystal etch	Crystal etch
Height	4$\frac{7}{16}$"	4$\frac{7}{16}$"	4$\frac{1}{2}$"
Price	$15.00	$15.00	$50.00

Company	Morgantown	Morgantown	Morgantown
Line	Unidentified	7590	7575
Pattern	Etch 272	Biscayne #747	American Beauty #734
Color	Crystal etch	Crystal etch	Crystal etch
Height	3$\frac{1}{16}$"	4$\frac{1}{16}$"	4$\frac{3}{8}$"
Price	$50.00	$60.00	$75.00

Company	Morgantown	Morgantown	Morgantown
Line	7630 Ballerina	7640 Art Moderne	808 Mikado
Pattern	Sunrise Medallion 758	762 Artic	Callahan 7711
Color	Crystal etch	Crystal etch	Crystal etch
Height	5$\frac{1}{8}$"	4$\frac{3}{8}$"	4$\frac{3}{8}$"
Price	$100.00	$85.00	$40.00

Stem #3 is the Candlewick pattern used for all gold decorated Candlewick. Is there a gold cordial? One can hope! An unusual adornment, #6 has three rose stems adorning the stem of this cordial.

99

Crystal Etch

Company	New Martinsville	New Martinsville	Tiffin
Line	4901	4902	
Pattern	Prelude	Prelude	Thistle
Color	Crystal etch	Crystal etch	Crystal etch
Height	4⁹⁄₁₆"	2⅞"	3½"
Price	$45.00	$45.00	$30.00

Company	Tiffin	Tiffin	Tiffin
Line	14179	14185	15024
Pattern	Dolores	Classic	Flanders
Color	Crystal etch	Crystal etch	Crystal etch
Height	3½"	4"	5⅛"
Price	$25.00	$45.00	$50.00

Company	Tiffin	Tiffin	Tiffin
Line	15037	15065	15066
Pattern	Byzantine	Cadena	Alahambra
Color	Crystal etch	Crystal etch	Crystal etch
Height	4⁹⁄₁₆"	5⅜"	4½"
Price	$40.00	$55.00	$50.00

Stems #1 and #2 are both Prelude cordials. I had a more difficult time finding #2. This is a pattern that few dealers recognize; so it is possible to find it at a bargain price once in a while.

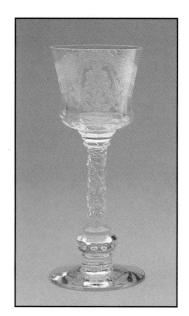

Crystal Etch

Company	Tiffin	Tiffin	Tiffin
Line	15067	15083	17043
Pattern	Cordelia	Fuschia	Cherokee Rose
Color	Crystal etch	Crystal etch	Crystal etch
Height	4¾"	4"	5³⁄₁₆"
Price	$40.00	$35.00	$40.00

Company	Tiffin	Tiffin	Tiffin
Line	17392	17392	15071
Pattern	June Night	Persian Pheasant	Cerice
Color	Crystal etch	Crystal etch	Crystal etch
Height	5⅛"	5⅛"	5⅛"
Price	$40.00	$60.00	$30.00

Company	Tiffin	Tiffin	Tiffin
Line	17399	17457	17474
Pattern	Cherokee Rose	Fuschia	Damask Rose
Color	Crystal etch	Crystal etch	Crystal etch
Height	5⅜"	5⅜"	3½"
Price	$40.00	$85.00	$25.00

Stem #1 is Tiffin Cordelia etch and so is #1 on page 105. This later one was not identified until late; so it is out of numerical order. It happened!

  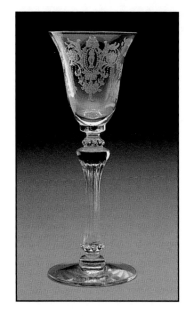

  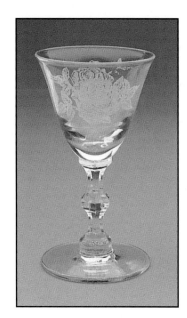

Crystal Etch and Frosted

Company	Tiffin	Unidentified	Bryce
Line	15047	Unidentified	854
Pattern	Cordelia	Unidentified	Unidentified
Color	Crystal etch	Crystal etch	Crystal etch
Height	4¼"	3½"	4½"
Price	$35.00	$12.00	$18.00

Company	Unidentified	Unidentified	Unidentified
Line	Unidentified	Unidentified	Unidentified
Pattern	Unidentified	Unidentified	Unidentified
Color	Crystal etch	Crystal etch	Crystal etch
Height	4"	3¹⁄₁₆"	4⅜"
Price	$20.00	$15.00	$15.00

Company	Cambridge	Fostoria	Fostoria
Line	7967	4024	4024
Pattern	Dawn	Victorian	Victorian
Color	Crystal frosted	Crystal frosted	Crystal frosted foot
Height	3⁵⁄₁₆"	3"	3"
Price	$45.00	$20.00	$20.00

I need some help identifying etches #2, #4, #5, and #6 on this page.

Crystal Frosted and Gold Decorated

Company	Heisey	Unidentified	Cambridge
Line	5058	Unidentified	3121
Pattern	Goose	Star cut	Rose Point Brandy
Color	Crystal frosted	Crystal frosted	Crystal gold encrusted
Height	5¾"	3⅝"	3¹⁵⁄₁₆"
Price	$180.00	$12.00	$135.00

Company	Cambridge	Cambridge	Cambridge
Line	3122	3500	3500
Pattern	Diane	Rose Point	Rose Point
Color	Crystal gold encrusted	Crystal gold foot	Crystal gold encrusted
Height	4¹⁵⁄₁₆"	5"	5"
Price	$75.00	$90.00	$95.00

Company	Cambridge	Economy	Economy
Line	3600	Band #10	#25 border
Pattern	Chantilly	Unidentified	Unidentified etch
Color	Crystal gold encrusted	Gold Decorated	Gold Decorated etch
Height	5"	3⁹⁄₁₆"	3¹⁵⁄₁₆"
Price	$80.00	$25.00	$25.00

Stems #5 and #6 illustrate the difference between Cambridge's gold decorated and gold encrusted. The workmanship on gold encrusted pieces made these more expensive both then and now. Gold decorations were 22K or 24K gold. Alas! There is not enough gold on these pieces to make them worth substantially more as some uninformed dealers seem to think!

  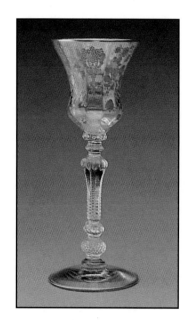

Crystal Gold Decorated

Company	Fostoria	Glastonbury Lotus	Imperial
Line	Etch 250	78	3400
Pattern	Oriental Design	Unidentified	Candlewick
Color	Gold Decorated etch	Gold Decorated etch	Crystal Frosted w/gold
Height	3⁷⁄₁₆"	3¹⁵⁄₁₆"	4½"
Price	$50.00	$25.00	$65.00

Company	Libbey	Tiffin	Unidentified
Line	3003	17594	Unidentified
Pattern	Golden Foliage #8990	Pa Lais Versailles	Unidentified
Color	Crystal w/gold oak leaves	Crystal w/gold	Gold Decorated etch
Height	3⁵⁄₁₆"	5⁵⁄₁₆"	3⁵⁄₈"
Price	$5.00	$95.00	$20.00

Company	Unidentified	Unidentified	Unidentified
Line	Unidentified	Unidentified	Unidentified
Pattern	Unidentified	Unidentified	Unidentified
Color	Gold Decorated etch	Gold Decorated	Gold Decorated
Height	3¹⁵⁄₁₆"	3⅜"	4⁷⁄₁₆"
Price	$20.00	$20.00	$20.00

Stem #1 gave Cathy and me fits trying to identify it from our working photo until I realized that the photographer had missed viewing the bird! It was turned so you could only see a partial tail. Stem #5 is a late version of Tiffin's Cherokee Rose with gold, yet is a separate pattern.

Crystal with Paint, Platinum, and Silver

Company	Unidentified	Unidentified	Tiffin
Line	Unidentified	Unidentified	17356
Pattern	Enameled Flowers	Jumping Horse	Melrose
Color	Crystal/painted	Crystal/painted	Crystal etch plat. band
Height	4⅛"	4¹⁄₁₆"	4⁵⁄₁₆"
Price	$15.00	$15.00	$45.00

Company	Cambridge	Tiffin	Libbey
Line	3122	15042	3002
Pattern		Athens	"Silver Foliage"
Color	Crystal platinum edge	Crystal platinum	Silver
Height	4⅞"	3¹⁵⁄₁₆"	4³⁄₁₆"
Price	$45.00	$35.00	$5.00

Company	Unidentified	Cambridge	Cambridge
Line	Unidentified	Chantilly Crystal sterling	Rose Point Crystal Wal-
Pattern	Diane & Cupid	Base weighted	Lace sterling base
Color	Silver Decorated	Sterling stem	Sterling stem
Height	4¹⁄₁₆"	3½"	3⅜"
Price	$30.00	$75.00	$325.00

Stem #7 has caused me many hours of research thus far, all in vain. I have four cordials with this pattern on three different stems, one in yellow. One was bought as Paden City, one as Tiffin, and another as Lotus. Can you confirm the maker of any of these? Stems #8 and #9 are both Cambridge with sterling bases. Notice (from the price) that Rose Point is about four times as desirable as Chantilly.

 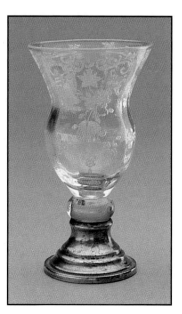 

Green

Company	Anchor Hocking	Cambridge	Cambridge
Line		1066 no optic	1066 optic
Pattern	Colonial	Aurora	Aurora
Color	Green	Forest green	Emerald
Height	3¹³⁄₁₆"	3⅞"	3⅞"
Price	$28.00	$40.00	$40.00

Company	Cambridge	Cambridge	Cambridge
Line	1400	1402	1402/100
Pattern	Martha Washington	Tally Ho	Tally Ho
Color	Forest green	Forest green	Forest green
Height	3¹⁄₁₆"	2⅝"	5"
Price	$50.00	$50.00	$60.00

Company	Cambridge	Cambridge	Cambridge
Line	300	3011/14	3075
Pattern	Caprice	Statuesque	Imperial Hunt scene
Color	Pistachio	Forest green	Light emerald
Height	4⅜"	5⅞"	3¾"
Price	$275.00	$400.00	$175.00

Stem #7 brings back memories of my failure to buy six of these when I had a chance. I only bought one for my collection and have never seen another for sale in over ten years!

  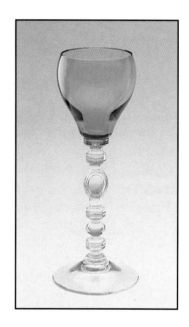

  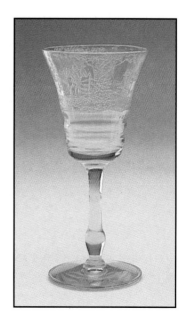

Green

Company	Cambridge	Cambridge	Cambridge
Line	3121 no optic	3122	3126
Pattern	Portia		
Color	Forest green	Forest green	Forest green
Height	4¹⁵⁄₁₆"	4¹⁵⁄₁₆"	4¹⁵⁄₁₆"
Price	$225.00	$50.00	$60.00

Company	Cambridge	Cambridge	Cambridge
Line	1327	3130	3130
Pattern			Apple Blossom
Color	Pistachio	Light emerald	Light emerald
Height	3⁵⁄₁₆"	4⅜"	4⅜"
Price	$25.00	$45.00	$125.00

Company	Cambridge	Cambridge	Cambridge
Line	3575	3575	3105
Pattern	Stradivari/Regency	Stradivari/Regency	Rose Point Pressed
Color	Forest green	Pistachio	Forest green
Height	5⅜"	5⅜"	4⅝"
Price	$50.00	$50.00	$150.00

Stem #1 may be one of the rarest cordials pictured in this book although the price may not indicate that. Demand always supersedes rarity when it comes to pricing. In any case, don't pass any forest green Portia stems!

  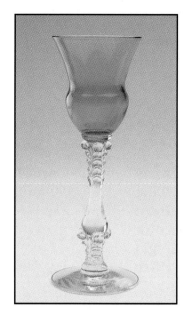

Green ───────────────────────────

Company	Dorflinger	Fostoria	Fostoria
Line	Unidentified	4024	5082
Pattern	Unidentified	Victorian	Mystic etch 270½
Color	Green cut	Empire Green	Green
Height	4"	3¹⁄₁₆"	3¹¹⁄₁₆"
Price	$60.00	$30.00	$60.00

Company	Fostoria	Fostoria	Fostoria
Line	5097	5098	5098
Pattern	Spartan etch 80	Acanthus etch 282	Versailles etch 278
Color	Green	Green	Green
Height	3½"	3⅞"	3⅞"
Price	$60.00	$55.00	$80.00

Company	Fostoria	Fostoria	Fostoria
Line	5412	6003	6011
Pattern	Colonial Dame		Neo Classic
Color	Empire green	Green	Empire green
Height	3¼"	3⁷⁄₁₆"	3³⁄₁₆"
Price	$25.00	$35.00	$40.00

Stem #1 was bought a few years ago from a set in a shop in Florida. I have only the testimony from those dealers that this is Dorflinger.

117

Green ─────────────

Company	Fostoria	Fry	Morgantown
Line	870		6046
Pattern	Seville etch 274	Swirl connector	Kirby
Color	Green	Green	Stiegel green
Height	3⁷⁄₁₆"	2¾"	3¹⁄₁₆"
Price	$70.00	$35.00	$40.00

Company	Morgantown	Morgantown	Morgantown
Line		7643	7643
Pattern	Hex	Golf Ball	Golf Ball
Color	Stiegel green filament	Meadow green	Meadow green stem
Height	3¹³⁄₁₆"	3⁷⁄₁₆"	3½"
Price	$55.00	$30.00	$60.00

Company	Morgantown	New Martinsville	New Martinsville
Line	7688½		
Pattern	Roanoke	Radiance	Moondrops
Color	Stiegel green	Green dark	Green dark
Height	3⁹⁄₁₆"	2⅝"	3"
Price	$40.00	$30.00	$28.00

Stem #7 is a Golf Ball stem that has a colored stem instead of bowl. This combination is rarely found in comparison to the crystal stems with colored bowls.

Green

Company	New Martinsville	Paden City	Steuben
Line		991	
Pattern	Moondrops	Penny Line	Threading
Color	Green light	Green light	Green
Height	3"	3⅜"	4⅜"
Price	$28.00	$15.00	$175.00

Company	Tiffin	Tiffin	Tiffin
Line	15016	15074	17458
Pattern	Psyche		
Color	Green	Killarney	Killarney
Height	4¾"	5⅝"	3¾"
Price	$75.00	$25.00	$25.00

Company	Unidentified	Unidentified	Unidentified
Line		Unidentified	Unidentified
Pattern	Rooster head	Dolphin stem	Palm tree etch
Color	Green	Green	Green
Height	3⅜"	4½"	3⅝"
Price	$60.00	$100.00	$15.00

Stem #3 has been identified as Fry and as Steuben. I have been told by an expert that the best way to determine manufacture of these is to check the colored threading. If the threading is even and uniform, it is probably moulded and Fry. However, if the threading is uneven, it probably was hand done by Steuben. Also see page 37 #4.

Green

Company	Unidentified	Unidentified	Unidentified
Line	Unidentified	Unidentified	Unidentified
Pattern	Unidentified	Unidentified	Unidentified
Color	Green	Green base and swirled stem	Green w/cut crystal top
Height	5¾"	4⁹⁄₁₆"	3⅛"
Price	$18.00	$20.00	$20.00

Company	Unidentified	Unidentified	Unidentified
Line	Unidentified	Unidentified	Unidentified
Pattern	Unidentified	Unidentified	Unidentified
Color	Green stem w/etched flower	Green Pistachio	Green
Height	3⅛"	3⅞"	4⅜"
Price	$20.00	$18.00	$15.00

Company	Unidentified	Unidentified	Unidentified
Line	Unidentified	Unidentified	Unidentified
Pattern	Unidentified	Unidentified	Unidentified
Color	Green	Green	Green cut
Height	3¹³⁄₁₆"	4"	3⅛"
Price	$18.00	$18.00	$20.00

This page illustrates nine green stems that baffled all my helpers. If you recognize any of these, let us know!

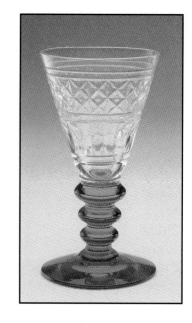

Iridized and Metallic

Company	Fostoria	Heisey	Heisey
Line	6024	3390	3390 2½ oz. wine
Pattern	Coral Pearl	Carcassone	Carcassone
Color	Iridized	Iridized/yellow flashed	Iridized
Height	3¾"	2¾"	3"
Price	$30.00	$30.00	$20.00

Company	Libbey	Steuben	Unidentified
Line	Silhoutte	Unidentified	Unidentified
Pattern	Greyhound	Unidentified	Unidentified
Color	Opal	Pearlized	Iridescent
Height	4"	3⁹⁄₁₆"	4⅜"
Price	$200.00	$250.00	$12.00

Company	Fostoria	Unidentified	Cambridge
Line	6005	Unidentified	Faberware
Pattern		Unidentified	Metallic stem
Color	Mother of Pearl/topaz	Iridized Swirled	Amethyst
Height	3¾"	3¹¹⁄₁₆"	2⅝"
Price	$18.00	$15.00	$20.00

Stems #2 and #3 are pieces of Heisey from New England that have a non-factory finish. You can find #8 in other colors.

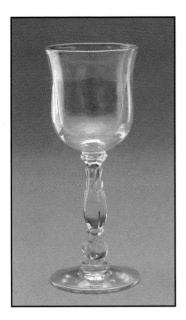

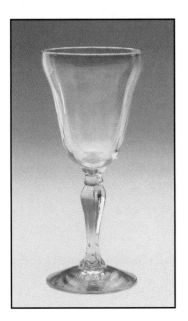

Metallic

Company	Cambridge	Cambridge	Cambridge
Line	Faberware	Faberware	Faberware
Pattern	Metallic stem	Metallic stem	Metallic stem
Color	Amethyst	Royal blue	Crystal
Height	4¼"	4¼"	4¼"
Price	$20.00	$25.00	$20.00

Company	Cambridge	Cambridge	Cambridge
Line	Faberware	Faberware	Faberware
Pattern	Metallic stem	Metallic stem	Metallic stem
Color	Milk	Carmen	Carmen
Height	4¼"	4¼"	2⅞"
Price	$30.00	$25.00	$25.00

Company	New Martinsville	New Martinsville	New Martinsville
Line	Moondrops	Moondrops	No. 38
Pattern	Metallic stem	Metallic stem	Metallic stem
Color	Amethyst	Red	Red
Height	4"	4"	4"
Price	$55.00	$60.00	$30.00

Cambridge and New Martinsville seemed to corner the market on stems using metallic holders. None of these are considered hard to find, but many collectors enjoy the metallic accents.

Pink

Company	Anchor Hocking	Cambridge	Cambridge
Line		1327	1327
Pattern	Mayfair		
Color	Pink	LaRosa	Peach Blo
Height	3¾"	3⁵⁄₁₆"	3⁵⁄₁₆"
Price	$1,000.00	$25.00	$22.00

Company	Cambridge	Cambridge	Cambridge
Line	1341	3060	3075
Pattern	Mushroom	703 etch	Imperial Hunt scene
Color	LaRosa	Peach Blo	Peach Blo/gold encrust
Height	1¹³⁄₁₆"	3¾"	3¹¹⁄₁₆"
Price	$12.00	$60.00	$250.00

Company	Cambridge	Cambridge	Cambridge
Line	3077	3130	3135
Pattern		Gloria	Apple Blossom
Color	Peach Blo	Peach Blo	Peach Blo
Height	3¾"	4⅜"	4½"
Price	$45.00	$135.00	$125.00

Stem #1 is the most expensive cordial in this book. I remember a dealer setting up at Washington Court House, Ohio, for over a year with eight of these for $300.00 each. The catch was that you had to buy all eight. I have often wondered what happened to those cordials!

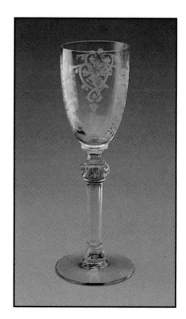

Pink

Company	Cambridge	Fostoria	Fostoria
Line	3575	5097	5098
Pattern	Stradivari/Regency		June etch 279
Color	LaRosa	Rose	Rose
Height	5⅜"	3½"	3⅞"
Price	$45.00	$30.00	$150.00

Company	Fostoria	Fostoria	Imperial
Line	5098	5099	
Pattern	Versailles etch 278	Fairfax	Pillar Flutes
Color	Rose	Rose	Pink
Height	3⅞"	3⅞"	3³⁄₁₆"
Price	$80.00	$35.00	$35.00

Company	Morgantown	Morgantown	New Martinsville
Line	7643	7643	
Pattern	Golf Ball	Golf Ball	Moondrops
Color	Anna Rose	Anna Rose cut	Pink
Height	3⁷⁄₁₆"	3⁷⁄₁₆"	3"
Price	$30.00	$30.00	$28.00

Stem #3 was one of the most difficult Fostoria cordials to find. Everyone has these in blue. Pink is not often found!

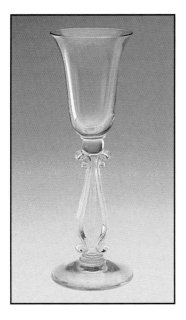

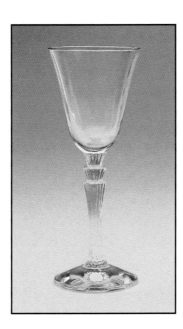

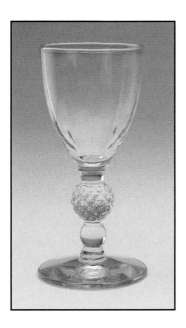

Pink and Purple-Pink

Company	Tiffin	Tiffin	Tiffin
Line	15024	15024	15033
Pattern	Arcadian	Flanders	Fontaine
Color	Pink	Rose	Rose
Height	5⅛"	5⅛"	5⅛"
Price	$35.00	$100.00	$90.00

Company	Tiffin	Tiffin	Fry (?)
Line	17051	17394	Unidentified
Pattern			Double squared stem
Color	Wisteria	Wisteria	Pink
Height	5"	2¹³⁄₁₆"	4⁵⁄₁₆"
Price	$35.00	$25.00	$20.00

Company	Cambridge	Cambridge	Central
Line	3035	3035	
Pattern		Gloria	
Color	Heatherbloom	Heatherbloom	Lilac
Height	4¹⁵⁄₁₆"	4¹⁵⁄₁₆"	3½"
Price	$150.00	$250.00	$40.00

Stems #4 and #5 are Tiffin's late pink called Wisteria (not to be confused with their Twilight). This is confusing because Fostoria's purple-pink color was also called Wisteria, shown by #2 and #3 on page 135. The purple-pink changes color according to its lighting. These pieces show pink in natural light and bluish purple in artificial lighting! Cambridge called this color Heatherbloom shown in #7 and #8.

Purple-Pink

Company	Fostoria	Fostoria	Fostoria
Line	5097	5098	6003
Pattern	Spartan etch 80	Fairfax	
Color	Orchid	Wisteria	Wisteria stem
Height	3½"	3⅞"	3⅜"
Price	$45.00	$75.00	$45.00

Company	Fostoria	Heisey	Tiffin
Line	877	3390	15033
Pattern	Vernon etch 277	Carcassone	
Color	Orchid	Alexanderite	Twilight
Height	3¾"	2¾"	5¹⁄₁₆"
Price	$75.00	$210.00	$75.00

Company	Tiffin	Tiffin	Tiffin
Line	15033	17051	17595
Pattern	Fontaine		
Color	Twilight	Twilight	Twilight
Height	5⅛"	5"	3¹⁵⁄₁₆"
Price	$125.00	$40.00	$40.00

Heatherbloom (Cambridge), Wisteria (Fostoria), Alexanderite (Heisey), and Twilight (Tiffin) are essentially the same color. Each glass company gave a different name to their composition of this color. You can be completely fooled looking at stems under florescent light. I once had to ask if I could carry some Twilight stems outside to make sure they were what I thought they were.

Red

Company	Cambridge	Cambridge	Cambridge
Line		1066 no optic	1402/100
Pattern	Tuxedo	Aurora	Tally Ho
Color	Carmen foot	Carmen	Carmen
Height	1¾"	3⅞"	5"
Price	$22.00	$45.00	$65.00

Company	Cambridge	Cambridge	Cambridge
Line	3011/14	3035	3078
Pattern	Statuesque		
Color	Carmen	Carmen	Carmen crystal ft.
Height	5⅞"	4¹⁵⁄₁₆"	3½"
Price	$495.00	$60.00	$50.00

Company	Cambridge	Cambridge	Cambridge
Line	3103	3104	3122
Pattern			
Color	Carmen	Carmen	Carmen
Height	3⁵⁄₁₆"	7"	4¹⁵⁄₁₆"
Price	$50.00	$325.00	$60.00

Stem #8 was one cordial I had to borrow for this book. Only a couple had ever been found and these came from a Cambridge worker's home. Those 7" stems must have been extremely delicate. I worried for a month about getting it back in one piece after I borrowed it for photography. Does anyone own a royal blue one?

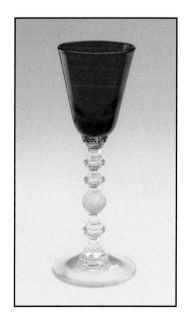

Red

Company	Cambridge	Canton	Duncan & Miller
Line	3500	#175	50
Pattern	Rose Point	Unidentified	Arliss
Color	Carmen gold encrusted	Red	Red
Height	5"	3⁷⁄₁₆"	3¼"
Price	$450.00	$30.00	$40.00

Company	Duncan & Miller	Fostoria	Fostoria
Line	5330	6011	6012
Pattern	Dover	Neo Classic	Westchester
Color	Red	Ruby	Ruby
Height	3⁹⁄₁₆"	3³⁄₁₆"	3⅜"
Price	$45.00	$45.00	$35.00

Company	Imperial	McKee	Morgantown
Line	3800		
Pattern	Candlewick	Rock Crystal	7616½ Wescott
Color	Ruby	Ruby	Spanish red filament
Height	3⁵⁄₁₆"	2⅞"	3⅝"
Price	$100.00	$60.00	$45.00

Stem #2 was found in a 1954 Canton catalog, but may have come from Paden City. Many of the items shown in this catalog were former Paden City products. (I even found many kitchenware items still being advertised in this catalog!)

Red

Company	Morgantown	Morgantown	Morgantown
Line	7617 Brilliant	7643	#7660½
Pattern		Golf Ball	Empress
Color	Spanish red	Spanish red	Spanish red
Height	4³⁄₁₆"	3⁷⁄₁₆"	4¾"
Price	$55.00	$40.00	$70.00

Company	Morgantown	Morgantown	Morgantown
Line	7684	7690 Monroe	
Pattern	Yale		Hex
Color	Spanish red	Spanish red	Spanish red filament
Height	4"	4¾"	3⅜"
Price	$160.00	$70.00	$50.00

Company	Morgantown	Morgantown	New Martinsville
Line			
Pattern	Hex	Hex	Radiance
Color	Spanish red filament	Spanish red filament	Red
Height	3⅞"	4½"	2⅝"
Price	$50.00	$50.00	$40.00

No stem line number has been found for the Hex stems of Morgantown. All Morgantown line numbers listed in this book are from Jerry Galagher's Morgantown book that can be found listed in the Bibliography of this book.

Red

Company	New Martinsville	Paden City	Paden City
Line		#90	991
Pattern	Moondrops	Chavalier	Penny Line
Color	Red/platinum	Red	Red
Height	3"	3⁷⁄₁₆"	3³⁄₈"
Price	$30.00	$30.00	$20.00

Company	Paden City	Unidentified	Unidentified
Line	991	Unidentified	Unidentified
Pattern	Penny Line	Twist stem	Vintage
Color	Red Dark	Red	Red w/gold
Height	3³⁄₈"	5⁵⁄₈"	2½"
Price	$20.00	$15.00	$20.00

Company	Bryce	Unidentified	Unidentified
Line	961	Unidentified	Unidentified
Pattern	Aquarius	Unidentified	Unidentified
Color	Red	Red flashed	Red
Height	3³⁄₈"	3¾"	3¾"
Price	$20.00	$12.00	$20.00

Stems #3 and #4 show two red #991 cordials. Stem #4 is so dark it looks black until illuminated brightly. Some collectors love this dark shade of red while others avoid it. That is one thing that makes collecting so interesting. Everyone has different ideas about what looks great!

Yellow

Company	Bryce	Bryce	Cambridge
Line	943	946	1066 optic
Pattern	Colonade	Delhi	Aurora
Color	Yellow	Yellow	Mandarin gold
Height	4⅜"	3½"	3⅞"
Price	$35.00	$18.00	$40.00

Company	Cambridge	Cambridge	Cambridge
Line	3035	3077	3120
Pattern		Cleo	Apple Blossom
Color	Gold Krystol	Gold Krystol	Gold Krystol
Height	4¹⁵⁄₁₆"	3¾"	4⅞"
Price	$50.00	$125.00	$90.00

Company	Cambridge	Cambridge	Cambridge
Line	3120	3121	3122
Pattern		Wildflower	
Color	Gold Krystol	Gold Krystol	Gold Krystol
Height	4¹⁵⁄₁₆"	5⅛"	4¹⁵⁄₁₆"
Price	$50.00	$125.00	$80.00

Stem #1 Colonade comes in several colors. These are rather majestic in appearance. Stem #3 shows Cambridge's Mandarin gold while all the rest of the Cambridge stems shown are Gold Krystol.

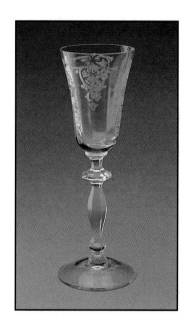

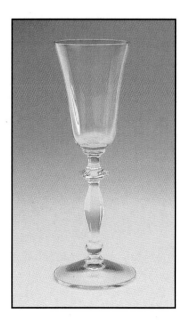

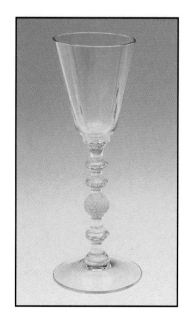

Yellow

Company	Cambridge	Cambridge	Cambridge
Line	3130	3135	3135
Pattern			Apple Blossom
Color	Gold Krystol	Gold Krystol	Gold Krystol
Height	4⅜"	4½"	4½"
Price	$45.00	$50.00	$100.00

Company	Cambridge	Fostoria	Fostoria
Line	3575	5098	5098
Pattern	Stradivari/Regency	Fairfax	June etch 279
Color	Gold Krystol	Topaz	Topaz
Height	5⅜"	3¹⁵⁄₁₆"	3¹⁵⁄₁₆"
Price	$40.00	$35.00	$70.00

Company	Fostoria	Fostoria	Heisey
Line	5099	5099	3380
Pattern	Trojan etch 280	Versailles etch 278	Old Dominion
Color	Topaz	Topaz	Sahara
Height	3⅞"	3⅞"	3⅝"
Price	$70.00	$65.00	$90.00

Cambridge yellow cordials might appear to be plentiful from looking at these pages, but you are looking at twenty years of buying cordials. I assure you they are not so commonly found.

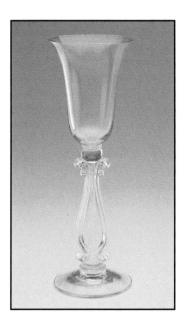

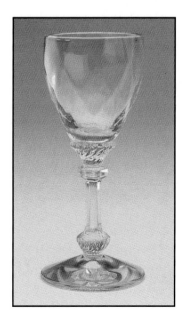

Yellow

Company	Heisey	Heisey	Heisey
Line	3381 Creole	3389 Duquense	3390
Pattern		Chintz	Carcassone
Color	Sahara	Sahara	Sahara
Height	3⅞"	4"	2¾"
Price	$200.00	$200.00	$75.00

Company	Heisey	Heisey	Lancaster
Line	3394	3416 Barbara Fritchie	
Pattern	Saxony		Jubilee
Color	Sahara	Sahara	Yellow
Height	2½"	5¹⁵⁄₁₆"	3⅞"
Price	$90.00	$350.00	$235.00

Company	Lotus	Morgantown	Morgantown
Line	#66 Line optic	7604 Princeton	7643
Pattern	#1011 Flanders	Adonis #751	Golf Ball
Color	Yellow	Topaz	Topaz
Height	3⅞"	4¼"	3⁷⁄₁₆"
Price	$30.00	$75.00	$30.00

Stem #6 is the only Lancaster cordial in this book. It is also one of the most difficult to find. (You may have read the story of how my wife bought this for my birthday, hid it, and forgot to give it to me until she was editing my book where I mentioned seeing one that was too expensive to buy. This is it!)

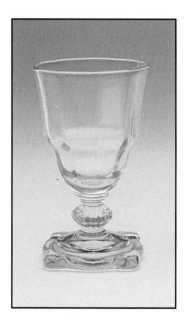  

Yellow

Company	Paden City	Seneca	Tiffin
Line	991	Unidentified	15024
Pattern	Penny Line	Ingrid	Lafleure
Color	Yellow	Yellow	Mandarin
Height	3⅜"	3¹⁄₁₆"	5⅛"
Price	$15.00	$20.00	$70.00

Company	Tiffin	Tiffin	Tiffin
Line	15037	15042	15047
Pattern	Byzantine		Flanders
Color	Mandarin	Mandarin (optic)	Mandarin
Height	4⁹⁄₁₆"	3¹⁵⁄₁₆"	4³⁄₁₆"
Price	$50.00	$30.00	$75.00

Company	Tiffin	Unidentified	Bryce
Line	15065	Unidentified	H2
Pattern	Cadena	Unidentified	Holiday
Color	Mandarin	Yellow	Yellow stem
Height	5⅜"	5⅜"	4⁷⁄₁₆"
Price	$85.00	$10.00	$15.00

Stem #9 was identified late causing it to be out of alphabetical order. I intend for any stems unidentified in this book to be updated in the next edition as new information surfaces!

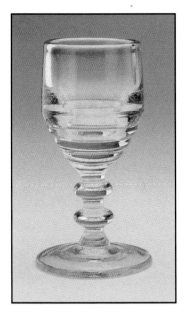

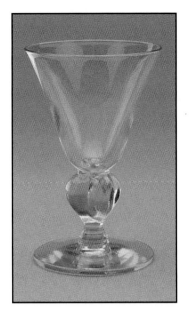

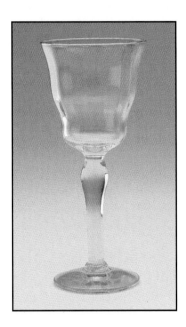

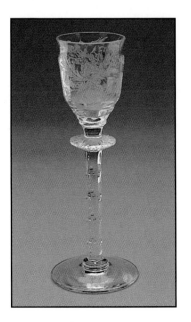

I had access to this set of Cambridge royal blue Statuesque stems thanks to Lynn Welker and Ralph Leslie. Ralph had one of the stems that Lynn was missing. Since I was working on a stemware book, it seemed like the ideal time to include them for recognition purposes. Many a brandy has been sold for cordial prices over the years. Look at the first two stems in the top row. The cordial is first and the brandy is second. Forget the minute difference in heights and note that they have distinctly different shapes. This alone could save you the price of this book! Maybe you can find a cordial priced as a brandy instead of vice versa. I am listing heights for each stem and a price range. The low end is for crystal, amber, amethyst, and forest green and the top range is for carmen and royal blue. These are the six colors in which cordials can be found. Height measurements will vary as much as ¼" due to mold changes or quality of craftmanship over the years.

Row 1:
1) Cordial   5¾" $400.00 – 500.00
2) Brandy   6" $90.00 – 140.00
3) V Cocktail   6⅜" $300.00 – 500.00
4) Cocktail   6⅜" $75.00 – 125.00
5) Wine   6½" $225.00 – 300.00
6) Tulip Cocktail   6½" $350.00 – 500.00
7) Sauterne   6½" $275.00 – 400.00

Row 2:
1) Ash Tray   6⅜" $175.00 – 250.00
2) Saucer Champagne   7¼" $125.00 – 150.00
3) Cigarette Box, short 7½" $175.00 – 300.00
4) Cigarette Holder   7½" $400.00 – 750.00
5) Claret   7⅝" $100.00 – 150.00

Row 3:
1) Blown Comport   7" $300.00 – 400.00
2) Hock   7¾" $300.00 – 400.00
3) Candleholder   9" $250.00 – 350.00
4) Cigarette Box, tall 9" $275.00 – 400.00
5) Table Goblet   9½" $135.00 – 175.00

Row 4:
1) Comport   9" $110.00 – 200.00
2) Sweetmeat   9½" $850.00 – 1250.00
3) Ivy Vase   9⅝" $125.00 – 200.00
4) Banquet Goblet   10" $250.00 – 400.00
5) Bud Vase   10⅛" $250.00 – 500.00

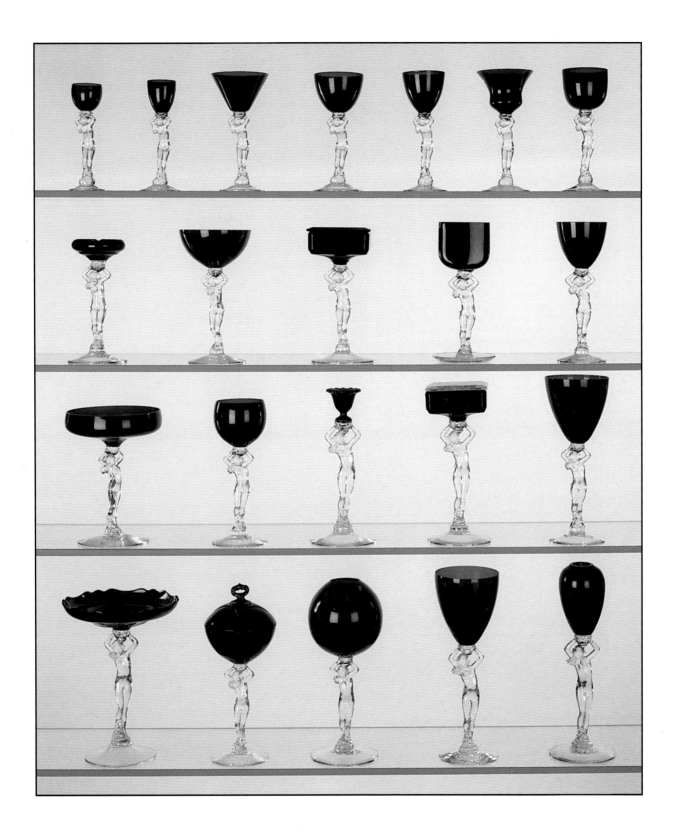

Cambridge Stems

I used Rose Point to illustate the shape of each piece of stemware and tumbler in a Cambridge pattern. Pay particular attention to the parfait and the juice tumbler as these are often confused. Since this book is basically one of identification, I felt that an example of the different pieces might prove valuable for beginners as well as anyone else having difficulty in distinguishing beverage items.

Row 1:
1) #3121 Water Goblet $30.00
2) #3121 Iced Tea Tumbler $32.50
3) #3121 Water Tumbler $29.00
4) #3121 Tall Sherbet $22.00
5) #3121 Cocktail $32.50
6) #3121 Short Sherbet $20.00
7) #3121 Oyster Cocktail $37.50

Row 2:
1) #968 Cocktail Icer $75.00
2) #3500 Claret $80.00
3) #3121 Parfait $75.00
4) #3121 Juice Tumbler $35.00
5) #3121 Wine $60.00
6) #3121 Cordial $70.00
7) #3500 Short Wine $57.50
8) #3121 Brandy $125.00

Fostoria Stems

I used Vesper to illustrate the shape of each piece of stemware and tumbler in a Fostoria pattern. Pay particular attention to the parfait and claret which are often confused since they are approximately the same height. The shapes are entirely different! That confusion should be eliminated using this picture as a reference. There are two pieces to the grapefruit shown last on the bottom row. Notice that the liner (which held the fruit) also has the pattern etched on it. Ice was placed in the larger bowl to chill the fruit placed in the liner!

Row 1:
1) #5093 Sherbet, low $17.00
2) #5093 Cocktail $27.50
3) #5093 Sherbet, high $17.50
4) #5093 Water Goblet $27.50
5) #5093 Parfait $40.00
6) #5093 Claret $75.00
7) #5093 Wine $37.50
8) #5093 Cordial $75.00

Row 2:
1) #5100 2 oz. Ftd. Bar $45.00
2) #5100 4 oz. Ftd. Oyster Cocktail $20.00
3) #5100 5 oz. Ftd. Juice $20.00
4) #5100 12 oz. Ftd. Tea $35.00
5) #5100 9 oz. Ftd. Water $20.00
6) #5082½ Grapefruit $50.00
6) #945½ Grapefruit Liner $45.00

Tiffin Stems

I have used Flanders to illustrate the shape of each piece of stemware and tumbler in a Tiffin pattern. There are three different water tumblers in the bottom row. I have never seen juice tumblers in this stem line although they do exist in some of Tiffin's other patterns.

Row 1:
1) Sherbet, high $17.50
2) Cocktail $40.00
3) Sherbet, low $28.00
4) Cordial $95.00
5) Claret $70.00
6) Parfait $85.00
7) Water Goblet $45.00

Row 2:
1) Grapefruit $100.00
2) 2½ oz. Ftd. Bar $80.00
3) 9 oz. Ftd. Water $22.00
4) 9 oz. Ftd. Water $40.00
5) 10 oz. Ftd. Water $45.00
6) 7 oz. Hdld. Parfait $150.00
7) 12 oz. Ftd. Tea $50.00

Bibliography

This is a partial compilation of the resources consulted by the author which actually provided useful references for the preparation of this book.

Archer, Margaret and Douglas, *Imperial Glass, 1904 – 1938.* Paducah, KY, Collector Books, 1978.

Bradley, Stephen & Constance S., and Robert Ryan, *Heisey Stemware.* Newark, OH, Spencer Walker Press, Inc., 1976.

Bredehoft, Neila, *The Collector's Encyclopedia of Heisey Glass 1925 – 1938.* Paducah, KY, Collector Books, 1986.

Bredehoft, Neila M. and Thomas H., *Handbook of Heisey Production Cuttings.* St. Louisville, OH, Cherry Hice Publications, 1991.

Emanuele, Concetta, *Stems.* Sunol, CA, Olive Tree Publications, 1970.

Fauster, Carl V., *Libbey Glass Since 1818.* Toledo, OH, Len Beach Press, 1979.

Gallagher, Jerry, *A Handbook of Old Morgantown Glass, Vol. I.* Minneapolis, MN, Merit Printing, 1995.

Genuine Duncan, Washington, PA, The Duncan & Miller Glass Co.

Handmade Duncan, The Lovliest Glassware in America, Cat. No. 89 Reprint, Washington, PA, The Duncan & Miller Glass Co.

H.C. Fry Glass Society, *The Collector's Encyclopedia of Fry Glassware.* Paducah, KY, Collector Books, 1990.

Koch, Nora, Reprint of 1916 Catalogue of Lead Blown Glassware. Otisville, MI, The Daze, 1984.

Long, Milbra and Emily Seate, *Fostoria Stemware, the Crystal for America.* Paducah, KY, Collector Books, 1995.

Miller, Everett R. and Addie R., *The New Martinsville Glass Story, Book II.* 1920 – 1950. Manchester, MI, Rymack Printing Co., 1975.

Nat'l Cambridge Collectors, Inc., *Colors in Cambridge Glass.* Paducah, KY, Collector Books, 1984.

Nat'l Cambridge Collectors, Inc. *Genuine Handmade Cambridge Fine Handmade Table Glassware 1949 thru 1953.* Paducah, KY, Collector Books, 1978.

Nat'l Cambridge Collectors, Inc., *Genuine Hand Made Cambridge Made in U.S.A.* Cambridge, OH, The Cambridge Glass Co.

Nye, Mark, *Cambridge Stemware, II.* Cambridge, OH, Nat'l Cambridge Collectors, Inc., 1994.

Page, Bob and Dale Frederiksen, *A Collection of American Crystal.* Greensboro, NC, Page-Frederiksen Publishing Co., 1995.

Page, Bob and Dale Fredriksen, *Seneca Glass Company 1891 – 1983.* Greensboro, NC, Page-Frederiksen Publishing Co., 1995.

Page, Bob and Dale Frederiksen, *Tiffin is Forever.* Greensboro, NC, Page-Frederiksen Publishing Co., 1994.

Replacements, Ltd., *Crystal Identification Guide.* Greensboro, NC

Stout, Sandra McPhee, *The Complete Book of McKee Glass.* N. Kansas City, MO, Trojan Press, Inc., 1972.

Walker, Mary Lyle and Lynn, *The Cambridge Glass Co.* Newark, OH, Spencer Walker Press, 1974.

Weatherman, Hazel Marie, *Colored Glassware of the Depression Era II.* Springfield, MO, Weatherman Glassbooks, 1974.

Weatherman, Hazel Marie, *Fostoria, Its First Fifty Years.* Springfield, MO, The Weathermans, 1972.

Index

Books By Gene Florence

Collector's Encyclopedia of Akro Agate Glassware $14.95
Collector's Encyclopedia of Depression Glass...$19.95
Collectible Glassware from the 40's 50's 60's $19.95
Pocket Guide to Depression Glass $9.95
Occupied Japan Price Guide Vol. 1 – 5..$9.95
Collector's Encyclopedia of Occupied Japan I $14.95
Collector's Encyclopedia of Occupied Japan II $14.95
Collector's Encyclopedia of Occupied Japan III $14.95
Collector's Encyclopedia of Occupied Japan IV...$14.95
Collector's Encyclopedia of Occupied Japan V..$14.95
Elegant Glassware of the Depression Era $19.95
Kitchen Glassware of the Depression Years $19.95
Very Rare Glassware of the Depression Years Third Series $24.95
Very Rare Glassware of the Depression Years Fourth Series......................................$24.95
Very Rare Glassware of the Depression Years Fifth Series..$24.95
Stemware Identification $24.95

Copies of these books may be ordered from:

Gene Florence   or   **Collector Books**
P.O. Box 22186   P.O. Box 64   P.O. Box 3009
Lexington, KY 40522   Astatula, Florida 34705   Paducah, KY 42002-3009

Add $2.00 postage for the first book, 30¢ for each additional book.

A Publication I Recommend

DEPRESSION GLASS DAZE

P.O. Box 576F, Otisville, MI 48463

A monthly newspaper devoted to the collecting of colored glass (depression glass & china) – features ads, articles, prices, news pertaining to this hobby. (12 issues)

Name _____

Address _____

City _____State ____Zip _____

☑*Please check one:*

❑ New
❑ 1 Yr. $21.00   ❑ Free Sample Copy
❑ 2 Yrs. $40.00   ❑ Canada $22.00

Club Information

Heisey Collectors of America
P.O. Box 27GF
Newark, OH 43055

Dues: $22 yearly

National Cambridge Collectors Inc.
P.O. Box 416 GF
Cambridge, OH 43725

Dues: $17 Individual
$3 Each Associate

Morgantown Collectors Guild
c/o Jerry Gallagher
420 First Ave. NW
Dept. GF
Plainview, MN 55964
Dues: $18 yearly

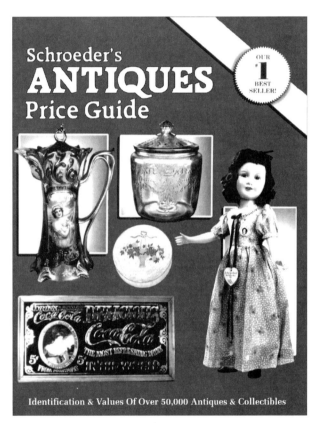